Grand Slams!

Grand Slams!

THE ULTIMATE COLLECTION OF BASEBALL'S BEST QUIPS, QUOTES, AND CUTTING REMARKS

Glenn Liebman

CONTEMPORARY BOOKS

Library of Congress Cataloging-in-Publication Data

Liebman, Glenn.
    Grand slams! : the ultimate collection of baseball's best
quips, quotes, and cutting remarks / Glenn Liebman.
        p.   cm.
    ISBN 0-8092-9731-0
    1. Baseball—United States—Humor.   2. Baseball—United
States—Quotations, maxims, etc.   I. Title: Ultimate collection
of baseball's best quips, quotes, and cutting remarks.   II. Title.
GV867.3.L55   2000
796.357—dc21   00-55504
                                                                    CIP

Interior design by Monica Baziuk

Published by Contemporary Books
A division of NTC/Contemporary Publishing Group, Inc.
4255 West Touhy Avenue, Lincolnwood (Chicago), Illinois 60712-
1975 U.S.A.
Printed in the United States of America
International Standard Book Number: 0-8092-9731-0
01 02 03 04 05 06 LB 14 13 12 11 10 9 8 7 6 5 4 3 2 1

To Frankie,
my all-time favorite T-ball player

Acknowledgments

I WOULD LIKE TO THANK the many hilarious people involved in the sport of baseball who made this book so enjoyable to put together. I would also like to thank the people at NTC/Contemporary, who have been wonderful to work with over the last several years—John Nolan, Denise Betts, and Craig "Mr. Never Give Up on the White Sox" Bolt.

In recent years, I have made friends with some wonderful people in the mental health field. Few combine intelligence and compassion better than my friend John "Mr. Never Give Up on the Giants" Tauriello.

I can't put together a baseball book without mentioning my close friend and fanatical Yankees fan, Scott Sommer.

I would also like to thank my dad, Bernie, who has told me many a story about baseball in the glory days (defined as when the Dodgers still played in Brooklyn); my late mother, Frieda (who stayed on the line for six hours so my brother and I could get tickets to Game 5 of the '69 Series); and my brother, Bennett, who took me to my first game (where I missed a Dick Allen foul ball by inches) and countless others since then.

Finally, I would like to thank the best double-play combo there ever was. The hard-hitting five-year-old, the terror of T-ball, the person who has helped make life great every day—my son, Frankie, and the other member of the team who is responsible for making the last 17 years so terrific (the only person besides my brother and father who can document that I once had a full head of hair)—my wonderful wife, Kathy.

Introduction

THE BASEBALL INSULT is as old as the game itself. You can just imagine Abner Doubleday ribbing the opposition at Cooperstown Stadium.

Baseball quips are as legendary as the great players of the game. Who can forget Graig Nettles's famous line about Yankees teammate and friend Sparky Lyle, who was traded from the Yankees a year after winning the Cy Young Award—"From Cy Young to sayonara."

Almost no player, manager, owner, commissioner, stadium, or team is spared from the barbs in this book. Name the team, and whether they have a lasting legacy of greatness, like the Yankees (former GM Bob Quinn, on their many managerial changes—"The two biggest expenses for Yankee employees—coming and going-away parties"), or of futility, like the old Washington Senators (sportswriter Roger Kahn on the Senators—"For the

Washington Senators, the worst part of the year is the baseball season"), they are likely to be featured in this compendium of baseball insults.

Every baseball subject you can imagine is also featured in this book. Whether it's passed balls (former Giants announcer Hank Greenwald, on the four passed balls of catcher Mark Salas—"You know you're in trouble when you say, 'Nice catch,' and it's the catcher you're talking about'), Dear Old Dad (Bob Uecker on his father—"I signed with the Milwaukee Braves for $3,000. That bothered my dad at the time, because he didn't have that kind of dough to pay out. But eventually he scraped it up"), or the fastball (Larry Andersen, on throwing a fastball after an injury—"I tried to throw cheese [fastball], but it wasn't a sharp cheddar. It was more like a soft Brie"), you will come away with a smile on your face.

So relax, take in your favorite 16–10 game (and those are the pitchers' ballparks), and enjoy your favorite nasty and funny one-liners.

Grand Slams!

Act Your Age

"It's nice to have a guy that young come along. We usually go out and find somebody who's 47."

—SPARKY ANDERSON, *on 25-year-old Tigers prospect John Doherty*

"There are younger Aztec ruins."

—BILL CONLIN, *on the ancient Vicente Romo*

"Tommy John is so old, he uses Absorbine Senior."

—BOB COSTAS

"Not only will I be changing diapers at home, now I will be changing them in the clubhouse."

> —JIM EISENREICH, *on his wife giving birth while he was playing on a young Florida Marlins team*

"When you're older than the manager and the general manager, that's not a good sign."

> —MIKE GALLEGO, *at age 35, rehabbing in Class A*

"That's one you can tell your grandchildren about—tomorrow."

> —RICK HORTON, *to 39-year-old Jerry Reuss after Reuss won his 200th game*

"When I broke in, they didn't have bats. We just grabbed the branch off a tree."

> —CHARLIE HOUGH

"I'd like to think that, but some of these guys are so young, I'm not sure they know whether Cleveland is in Ohio or Indiana."

> —TOM KELLY, *when asked if his young Twins team would gain valuable experience by losing a close game to the Indians*

"The average age of our bench is deceased."

> —TOMMY LASORDA, *on supersubs Manny Mota and Vic Davalillo*

"When you're 21, you're a prospect. When you're 30, you're a suspect."

> —JIM MCGLOTHLIN

"Other than that, I've been fine."

> —JOHNNY MIZE, *at age 79, about not playing in an old-timers' game because he had had a bypass operation, a knee replaced, cataracts, and prostate problems*

"The fans asked if I have any black-and-white tape of me when I first came into the league."

> —PAUL MOLITOR, *during his last year in the pros*

"I just hope I'm still walking when I'm 40 years old."

> —MIKE PIAZZA, *amazed at pros who are playing in their 40s*

"I'll never make the mistake of being 70 again."

> —CASEY STENGEL

"I didn't see [Christy] Mathewson, but Oquendo said he had a good slider."

> —BOB TEWKSBURY, *poking fun at the ageless Jose Oquendo*

"There are no fresh tires in my body. I'm that foam plus that you buy at the local auto store just to get to the next station."

> —ANDY VAN SLYKE, *attempting a comeback at age 36*

Ads

"I was offered a spot in an ad for neutering pets. Not exactly what I had in mind."

> —STEVE BEDROSIAN, *on trying to capitalize on his popularity after winning the Cy Young Award*

"Sporting goods companies pay me not to endorse their products."

> —BOB UECKER

Agents

"A complete ballplayer today is one who can hit, field, run, throw, and pick the right agent."

—BOB LURIE, *former owner of the Giants*

"When they smile, blood drips off their teeth."

—TED TURNER, *on agents*

Mike Aldrete

"It was better than a couple years I had."

—MIKE ALDRETE, *on how it felt to have a five-RBI game*

Dick Allen

"I wouldn't give him a high fastball or a fast highball."

—GENE MAUCH, *on Dick Allen*

"Play him, fine him, and play him again."

—GENE MAUCH, *on Dick Allen*

All-Star Game

"The only thing bad about winning the pennant is that you have to manage the All-Star Game the next year. I'd rather go fishing for three days."

—WHITEY HERZOG

"It's amazing the fans want to see me play. It's kind of scary. I guess that's what's wrong with our society."

—JOHN KRUK, *'93 All-Star Game starter*

"It's a lousy job. No matter what you pick, you're gonna be condemned."

—BILLY MARTIN, *on being an All-Star Game manager*

Mike Anderson

"His limitations are limitless."

>—DANNY OZARK, *on Phillies outfielder Mike Anderson*

Sparky Anderson

"Sparky came here two years ago promising to build a team in his own image. Now the club is looking for small, white-haired infielders with .212 batting averages."

>—AL ACKERMAN, *Tigers announcer, on Sparky Anderson managing the Tigers*

Angels

"You wonder if you brought in Henry Aaron and Lefty Grove would it have made any difference."

>—TIM BELCHER, *on the '99 Angels*

"The champagne they have stored is getting more valuable every year."

> —JOHNNY CARSON, *on the Angels never winning the World Series*

"We don't have the fire here because we don't have the match."

> —REX HUDLER, *on the lack of leadership on the Angels*

"I'd rather play in hell than for the Angels."

> —ALEX JOHNSON

"They couldn't break a chandelier if they had batting practice in a hotel lobby."

> —BILL LEE, *on a poor-hitting Angels team*

"Our phenoms aren't phenomenating."

> —LEFTY PHILIPS, *Angels manager, on a bad year*

"They're like the American League all-star team, and that's their problem: the American League all-star team always loses."

> —DAN QUISENBERRY, *on the Angels having star players but no chemistry*

"Somebody said to me, 'You can't trade 25 guys.' I said, 'Why not?' "

> —TONY TAVARES, *Angels president, after a disappointing '99 season*

Angels Fans

"It's like every game is a road game."

> —BO JACKSON, *on the fans' lack of support for the Angels*

Arms

"It doesn't matter if his shoulder's sore. He doesn't throw anyone out anyway."

—SPARKY ANDERSON, *on Kirk Gibson having one assist in 298 attempts*

"Dead arms? I think it's dead brain cells. I don't think there's anything to it."

—BOB FELLER, *on current-day ballplayers complaining about sore arms*

Artificial Turf

"If a horse can't eat it, then I don't like it."

—DICK ALLEN, *on artificial turf*

"The major advantage is that I won't wake up feeling like I just played a football game."

—RICKY GUTIERREZ, *on going from playing on Astroturf in Houston to natural grass in Chicago after he was traded*

"It's like playing with marbles in a bathtub."

> —DAVE LEMONDS, *on the artificial turf in Kansas City*

"It will revolutionize baseball. It will open a whole new area of alibis for the players."

> —GABE PAUL, *on artificial turf entering the game of baseball*

A's

"Jose Canseco asked me if he could pitch. I told him I'd let him know in the bottom of the first."

> —SANDY ALDERSON, *Oakland A's general manager, on a bad A's pitching staff*

"We run our club like a pawnshop—we buy, we trade, we sell."

> —CHARLIE FINLEY, *on the A's during the Finley era*

"I wanted to get into baseball in the worst way, and that's exactly what I did."

> —CHARLIE FINLEY, *on owning the Kansas City Athletics*

Astrodome

"This is a tough park for the hitter when the air conditioner is blowing in."

> —BOB BOONE, *on the Astrodome*

Attendance Figures

"That's not a crowd, that's my shirt size."

> —HANK GREENWALD, *on 1,632 people showing up at Candlestick Park*

"It was the first time in history that everyone in the stands got a foul ball."

> —DAVE LAPOINT, *on that same game with 1,632 people in attendance*

"Some people have those games where you guess the number of people in the park. Here you have to identify them too."

> —LEE MAZILLI, *on a crowd at Three Rivers Stadium*

"This place was so empty, they could have held archery practice."

> —BILL PARCELLS, *on going to an Indians game with 3,225 people in attendance*

"Sometimes you walk onto the field and wonder if they've opened the gates."

> —R. J. REYNOLDS, *on the crowds at Three Rivers Stadium*

Attitude Adjustment

"I'm not in a running mood."

> —RICKEY HENDERSON, *before the Mets' home opener in 2000 when asked why he didn't want to play in the game*

"When you play with no sleeves, you can get rug burns."

> —GARY SHEFFIELD, *on not diving for a catchable ball in Pittsburgh*

Autographs

"Any ballplayer that doesn't sign autographs for little kids ain't an American. He's a Communist."

> —ROGERS HORNSBY

"It's not worth much today, but in five years it will be worth even less."

> —TOMMY LASORDA, *on his autograph*

"Kids should practice autographing baseballs. This is a skill that's often overlooked in Little League."

> —TUG MCGRAW

"It was fun until a kid came up to me and said, 'My dad says you're getting old, you're going to die, and your autograph will be valuable.' "

> —WARREN SPAHN, *about an autograph show*

"I love signing autographs. I'll sign anything but veal cutlets. My ballpoint pen slips on veal cutlets."

—CASEY STENGEL

Awards

"I've often thought that a lot of awards are made up just so you'll come to the dinner."

—MICKEY MANTLE

"We gave him $47 million. He can pick up his award."

—WILLIE MAYS, *after his godson, Barry Bonds, did not pick up the MVP Award*

"I want to thank all the pitchers who couldn't go nine innings and manager Dick Howser, who wouldn't let them go."

—DAN QUISENBERRY, *on being named Rolaids Fireman of the Year*

"I didn't get a lot of awards as a player. But they did have a Bob Uecker day off for me once in Philly."

—BOB UECKER

B

Bad Days

"Let's be honest. We're down by eight runs and all I'm thinking about at that point is getting back to the hotel by midnight, because that's when room service closes."

—JOHN KRUK, *on the Dodgers losing an eight-run lead to the Phillies in the ninth inning*

"I couldn't have driven Miss Daisy home today."

—ANDY VAN SLYKE, *on a tough day at the plate*

Bad Predictions

"Ted Williams never thought that I'm as good as I am."

—BRANT ALYEA

"This is the last All-Star Game I'll miss."

> —OIL CAN BOYD, *after being left off the '85 all-star team*

"I believe the sale of Ruth will ultimately strengthen the team."

> —HARRY FRAZEE, *Red Sox owner, on selling Babe Ruth to the Yankees*

"I believe from here on in, Wise will be more consistent than Carlton."

> —GIL HODGES, *after future Cy Young Award winner Steve Carlton was traded for Rick Wise*

"He'll never make anything more than a Triple-A ballplayer at best."

> —BRANCH RICKEY, *on Yogi Berra*

"Rozema has the makings of a 30-game winner."

> —FRANK ROBINSON, *on Dave Rozema*

"I'm close to being the superstar I used to be."

> —RUBEN SIERRA, *three days before he was released in spring training*

Balls

"Only when I'm pitching."

> —JIM SLATON, *when asked if baseballs were livelier in 1977*

Baltimore

"Baltimore's such a lousy town, Francis Scott Key went out in a boat to write 'The Star-Spangled Banner.'"

> —BILLY MARTIN

Banquets

"If this club wants somebody to play third, they've got me. If they want somebody to go to luncheons, they should hire George Jessel."

> —GRAIG NETTLES, *on being fined $500 for missing a fund-raising event*

Baseball Cards

"I've asked the bubble-gum people to change the back of my card to read, 'In Military Service' or 'Out to Lunch.' "

—CHARLIE KERFELD, *on a bad '87 season*

"All I know is that it used to take 43 Marv Throneberry cards to get one Carl Furillo."

—MARV THRONEBERRY

"I knew when my career was over. In 1965, my baseball card came out with no picture."

—BOB UECKER

Baseball Wisdom (or Lack Thereof)

"Grantland Rice, the great sportswriter, once said, 'It's not whether you win or lose, it's how you play the game.' Well, Grantland Rice can go to hell as far as I'm concerned."

—GENE AUTRY

"The reason baseball calls itself a game, I believe, is that it's too screwed up to be a business."

> —JIM BOUTON

"The trouble with the big leagues is that there aren't enough big leaguers."

> —JIMMY CANNON

"When I began playing the game, baseball was about as sentimental as a kick in the crotch."

> —TY COBB

"Haven't they suffered enough?"

> —BEANO COOK, *on the Iran hostages receiving lifetime passes to all major-league baseball stadiums*

"Baseball players are the weirdest of all. I think it's all that organ music."

> —PETER GENT, *former NFL player*

"This is our product. At some point, you have to stop begging people to watch."

> —JOHN HART, *Indians general manager, on all the promotions to get people back to the ballpark after the 1995 strike*

"Trying to understand a game like this is like trying to program your VCR."

> —ERIC HILLMAN, *on losing a game after giving up three runs in the eighth inning*

"Baseball is a lot like life. The line drives are caught, the squibblers go for base hits. It's an unfair game."

> —ROD KANEHL

"Baseball is simple. All you do is sit on your butt, spit tobacco, and nod at the stupid things your manager says."

> —BILL LEE

"If nobody screwed up, why would baseball be worth watching?"

> —DARRYL MOTLEY

"Baseball isn't a business; it's more like a disease."

>—WALTER O'MALLEY

"There is no homework."

>—DAN QUISENBERRY, *on the best thing about baseball*

"Sometimes all of us need to be reminded that this is just a kid's game. We just happen to be grown men playing it."

>—MIKE STANTON

"Hell, if this game was half as complicated as some of the writers make out it is, a lot of us boys from the farm would never have been able to make a living at it."

>—BUCKY WALTERS

"Baseball is like church. Many attend, but few understand."

>—WES WESTRUM

Baserunners

"What we need is a second-base coach."

> —GRAIG NETTLES, *on bad baserunning by the Yankees*

Bash Brothers

"There were only two Bash Brothers, and one's in Boston now. Maybe I can be a Bash Stepchild."

> —SCOTT BROSIUS, *on being called the new Bash Brother with Mark McGwire after Jose Canseco was traded to Boston*

Basketball

"The ball is too big, and there's no chance of a rainout."

> —ERIC HILLMAN, *6′10″ New York Mets pitcher, on why he didn't play basketball*

Bats

"I owe my success to expansion pitching, a short right-field fence, and my hollow bat."

  —NORM CASH

Batting Stance

"Because you don't get to hit in the bullpen."

  —BOB UECKER, *on why he did not alter his stance*

Albert Belle

"He's been very talkative. But it's usually under oath."

  —SANDY ALDERSON, *on Belle*

"Everybody has warts. Some are more visible than others."

  —MIKE HARGROVE, *on Belle*

Bench Strength

"I'm an eclipse player. You don't see me very often."

—BENNY AYALA

"I think I hold the record for most games watched, career."

—KURT BEVACQUA

"I'm being showcased on the bench. They have me sitting where people can see me."

—RON GARDENHIRE

"You can't get rich sitting on the bench, but I'm giving it a try."

—PHIL LINZ

"Play me or keep me."

—PHIL LINZ, *his mock trade demand*

"Look at that guy—can't hit, can't run, can't catch. Of course, that's why they gave him to us."

—CASEY STENGEL, *on a player being traded to the Yankees*

"That fellow plays the same position I do—the bench."

> —GEORGE THOMAS, *career backup player, on*
> *seeing the back of Johnny Bench's jersey*

Moe Berg

"Moe Berg could speak eight languages, and he couldn't hit in any of them."

> —TED LYONS, *on the scholarly Berg*

Kurt Bevacqua

"Let's be serious. How many clubs call for Kurt Bevacqua?"

> —JACK MCKEON, *when asked if contenders were*
> *calling up asking about the availability of Kurt*
> *Bevacqua*

Bobby Bonilla

"We have a pretty good 24-man roster right now."

> —BOBBY VALENTINE, *on not considering Bobby Bonilla part of the Mets even though he was technically still on the team*

Bowling

"All I can do is throw a baseball and throw a bowling ball."

> —JOHN BURKETT, *major-league pitcher, on not being a great athlete*

"I wound up my career with a lifetime .200 average, which tied me with [bowling legend] Don Carter."

> —BOB UECKER

Braves

"It probably wouldn't be that different from some games we did in the '70s."

>—SKIP CARAY, *on announcing a Braves game with replacement players*

"This would have been a good year to paint the seats."

>—GERALD PERRY, *on a season of poor attendance in Atlanta*

"They're a shelter, all right—a bomb shelter."

>—TED TURNER, *after being asked early in his ownership of the Braves if the team was a tax shelter*

"This losing streak is bad for the fans . . . but look at it this way. We're making a lot of people happy in other cities."

>—TED TURNER, *on a Braves losing streak*

Braves Fans

"Everyone in Atlanta is going to need elbow surgery after the game because they're all doing the Tomahawk Chop."

—ANDY VAN SLYKE

Brewers

"You are as good as your record. If your record's bad, you're a bad team."

—JEROMY BURNITZ, *on the last-place Milwaukee Brewers*

"We didn't want to weaken the rest of the league."

—FRANK LANE, *Brewers GM, on not making any trades*

"After the kind of year we had, I've got to touch all the bases."

> —BUD SELIG, *then owner of the Brewers, on an off-season vacation when he met the Pope and the Chief Rabbi of Jerusalem*

"I refuse to believe that the Red Sox are like the Milwaukee Brewers."

> —MO VAUGHN, *on being told the Red Sox were not making any player moves because they were a small-market team*

Broadcasters

"I've only been doing this 54 years. With a little experience, I might get better."

> —HARRY CARAY

"Let's check out the replay on that one."

> —JOHNNY PESKY, *doing radio play by play*

"When I hit .211."

> —BILL WHITE, *on when he started to seriously consider becoming an announcer*

Bobby Brown

"Bobby Brown reminds me of a fellow who's been hitting for 12 years and fielding one."

> —CASEY STENGEL, *on Bobby Brown being a lousy fielder*

Bill Buckner

"The last guy who ran as badly as Bill Buckner was Long John Silver."

> —MARK HEISLER

George W. Bush

"If he can't run for office any better than he runs the Texas Rangers, he don't have any advantage."

—ED MARTIN, *Texas Democratic chairman, on George W.'s run for governor of Texas*

"I just think it would be cool to know the dude in the White House."

—DARREN OLIVER, *Rangers pitcher, on why he would support George W. Bush for president*

Candlestick Park

"It's like playing a game on an aircraft carrier in the North Atlantic."

—RICH DONNELLY, *on Candlestick Park*

"At night, that place is a graveyard with lights."

—WHITEY HERZOG, *on Candlestick Park*

"Candlestick was built on the water. It should have been built under it."

—ROGER MARIS

"They say it wasn't a bad place except for the wind. That's like saying hell wouldn't be a bad place if it weren't for the heat."

—JERRY REUSS, *on Candlestick Park*

"You know, you'd say, 'I got it.' In Candlestick, you'd
say, 'Who wants it?' "

—PETE ROSE, *on a pop-up in Candlestick Park*

Jose Canseco

"I can't believe I came here to honor a man who went
1-for-17 in the World Series."

—JAN MURRAY, *comedian, during a roast for
Jose Canseco*

Cardinals

"We need just two players to be a contender—Babe
Ruth and Sandy Koufax."

—WHITEY HERZOG, *on a bad Cardinals team*

"I'm lucky—I've managed in two eras. I managed in
the lively batter era of last year and the dead-ball era
this year."

—WHITEY HERZOG, *on the anemic offense of the
Cardinals' 1986 team*

Catchers

"The wind always seems to blow against catchers when they are running."

—YOGI BERRA

"I'm the best catcher in baseball other than Johnny Bench—but he's retired, I think."

—JUNIOR ORTIZ

"There must be some reason why we're the only ones facing the other way."

—JEFF TORBORG, *on being a catcher*

Wes Chamberlain

"He's the least impressive Chamberlain since Neville."

—VIN SCULLY, *on the mental mistakes of Wes Chamberlain*

Cheating

"We don't cheat. And even if we did, I'd never tell you."

> —TOMMY LASORDA, *on accusations of the Dodgers cheating*

Chemistry Class

"Yeah, and we're missing a little geography and arithmetic around here, too."

> —WHITEY HERZOG, *on the bad chemistry between members of the Cardinals team he managed*

Chicago

"If every bad game I watched reduced the time I spent in purgatory, I would spend no time there at all."

> —JACK BRICKHOUSE, *on being an announcer for both the Cubs and the White Sox*

"I grew up in an age when we prayed the Cubs and White Sox would merge so we would have only one bad team in Chicago."

—TOM DREESEN, *comedian who grew up in Chicago*

"You know what they say about Chicago. If you don't like the weather, wait fifteen minutes."

—RALPH KINER

Cincinnati

"It's a good thing I stayed in Cincinnati for four years. It took me that long to learn how to spell it."

—ROCKY BRIDGES

Circus

"Why should I leave a circus to go to a fair?"

—GRAIG NETTLES, *who declined an invitation to attend a state fair when playing for the Yankees*

"We need to start checking that circus for ballplayers. There are some real athletes there."

—MARGE SCHOTT, *on the circus coming to Cincinnati*

Roger Clemens

"It was like Frank Sinatra opening for Bob Uecker."

—JOHN TRAUTWEIN, *Red Sox reliever, on replacing Roger Clemens in a game*

Cleveland

"I went through Cleveland once and it was closed."

—JAY JOHNSTONE

Bill Clinton

"He's in the wrong place if he's looking for votes."

> —TOM BRUNANSKY, *on presidential candidate Bill Clinton visiting a spring training site after proposing increased taxes on the wealthiest individuals*

"I don't like it a bit. I hope by the time I sign my contract, he quits."

> —JOSE RIJO, *on President Bill Clinton's proposed tax on high-income individuals*

Clothes Horse

"I may have to wear one in my next line of work."

> —LARRY ANDERSEN, *on learning late in his career how to tie a necktie*

Coach

"The best qualification a coach can have is being the manager's drinking buddy."

—JIM BOUTON

"The main quality a great third-base coach must have is to be a fast runner."

—ROCKY BRIDGES

"Coaching third with a pitcher on base is like being a member of the bomb squad. The thing could blow up in your face at any moment."

—ROCKY BRIDGES

"Hotels have maids. Baseball teams have coaches."

—JOSE MARTINEZ

"The coaching jobs have gone to the .250 hitters."

—JOHNNY MIZE

"The game sure has changed since I played."

> —JOHN WATHAN, *said minutes after retiring as a player to become a coach*

"Coaches are an integral part of any manager's team, especially if they are good pinochle players."

> —EARL WEAVER

College Ball

"I was shocked and surprised. I don't know how we scored a run."

> —ERIC DENNIS, *athletic director at Robert Morris, after the school lost a baseball game to a rival college 71–1*

"How you play the game is for college ball. When you're playing for money, winning is the only thing that matters."

> —LEO DUROCHER

Collision

"They're going to have to hang a bell around one of their necks."

> —LARRY HANEY, *Brewers coach, on teammates Brian Downing and Gary Pettis colliding twice within a few days*

Comeback Player of the Year

"This man deserves the Comeback Player of the Year Award for this game alone."

> —ROGER CRAIG, *on Bob Brenly making four errors in one game and then hitting the game-winning home run*

"There must be some mistake. I've never been away."

> —DICK DONOVAN, *on finishing second in the voting for the Comeback Player of the Year Award*

"Do they have that award in Japan?"

> —PEDRO GUERRERO, *on the possibility of his winning the Comeback Player of the Year Award after a bad year*

"You know what that award tells you. It tells you that you were terrible the year before."

> —RICK SUTCLIFFE

Comebacks

"Expansion's coming up, pitching is thin, and I'm left-handed."

> —TOM BROWNING, *explaining why he was attempting a comeback after being out of baseball for several years*

Commissioner

"I'm not very smart. I think I can prove that. Who would accept a job with Marge Schott's dog, Ted Turner, and George Steinbrenner as your boss?"

> —PETER UEBERROTH, *on becoming baseball commissioner*

"What did the search committee decide? Not to search."

> —BOBBY VALENTINE, *on interim commissioner Bud Selig becoming the full-time commissioner*

"Resign."

> —BILL VEECK, *on the first thing he would do if he became baseball commissioner*

Competition

"They were all against me, but I beat the bastards and left them in the ditch."

> —TY COBB, *on his opponents*

"This guy wants to knock your head in and you want to knock his head in."

> —ANDY MESSERSMITH, *on the relationship between a hitter and a pitcher*

Complete Games

"Your pitchers have more complete games than you do."

> —WHITEY HERZOG, *to Hal MacRae, who was thrown out of several games when managing the Royals*

Consultant

"If he had made me a consultant five minutes ago, my first recommendation would have been not to fire the manager."

> —JOHN WATHAN, *who was offered a consulting job by the Royals GM after being fired as the manager*

Contracts

"There should be a commonsense clause in his contract."

> —JIM FREY, *on pitcher Steve Trout falling off his bike and missing a start*

"I was so poor, my first contract was signed in dirt."

> —MEL HALL

"It has guarantees through the year 2020 or until the last *Rocky* movie is made."

> —DAN QUISENBERRY, *on his long-term contract with the Giants*

"I offered him a no-cut contract, except in case of death."

> —TED TURNER, *on negotiations with free agent Andy Messersmith*

Control Issues

"They want me to throw it over the plate, and I don't pitch that way."

—RICK OWNBEY

"I was so wild, I could have walked Manute Bol four times."

—WALT TERRELL

Coors Field

"When you get two outs, you're a long way from the dugout in this park."

—TERRY COLLINS, *on Coors Field*

"You can play for the three-run homer there a lot—like every inning."

—JOE GIRARDI, *on Coors Field*

"It's a college game, only they use aluminum bats when we use wood. No lead is safe."

> —TODD HUNDLEY, *on playing in Coors Field*

"Nothing surprises me here. When you come here and pitch, you'd better pack a lunch."

> —CURTIS LESKANIC, *Rockies pitcher*

"You don't manage here, you persevere."

> —JIM LEYLAND, *on Coors Field*

Country Western

"Garth Brooks should have stuck around. Maybe he'd be playing."

> —BRUCE BOCHY, *Padres manager, on a rash of injuries after Brooks played with the Padres in spring training*

"Charlie showed us he could hit three ways—left, right, and seldom."

> —JOE KLEIN, *Rangers GM, on Charlie Pride playing in a Rangers exhibition game*

"He starts in the hitting area slow, then slows it down even more."

> —MERV RETTENMUND, *analyzing Garth Brooks's swing*

Cows Come Home

"I didn't try too hard. I was afraid I'd get emotionally involved with the cow."

> —ROCKY BRIDGES, *after finishing second in a milking contest*

"They say happy cows give more milk, but they've basically told me I'm dog meat."

> —KIRK GIBSON, *on the Royals telling him he would be a backup near the end of his career*

"If they had trouble winning on the road, we could say that things will be different when the Cows come home."

> —WOODY PAIGE, Denver Post *columnist, urging that the Colorado team be called the Cows instead of the Rockies*

Bobby Cox

"I think he's had to manage this year, and he's doing a good job doing that."

> —BOBBY VALENTINE, *on Bobby Cox meriting consideration for the Manager of the Year Award*

Cubs

"Good things come to those who wait . . . and wait . . . and wait."

> —ERNIE BANKS, *the eternal optimist, on the Cubs*

"The Chicago Cubs are like Rush Street—a lot of singles but no action."

> —JOE GARAGIOLA

"It's like in golf when you play a par 3 right after a par 5."

> —STEVE GARVEY, *on playing against a tough Cardinals team after playing the Cubs*

Cubs Fans

"The Chicago Cubs fans are the greatest fans in baseball. They've got to be."

> —HERMAN FRANKS, *former Cubs manager*

"One thing you can learn as a Cubs fan: when you buy your ticket, you can bank on seeing the bottom of the ninth."

> —JOE GARAGIOLA

Curfew

"I got players with bad watches—they can't tell midnight from noon."

> —CASEY STENGEL, *on a curfew he imposed while managing the Yankees*

"He was either out pretty late or up pretty early."

> —CASEY STENGEL, *on Don Larsen wrapping his car around a telephone poll at 5 A.M. during spring training*

"Anybody who can find something to do in St. Petersburg at five in the morning deserves a medal, not a fine."

> —CASEY STENGEL, *when asked if he was going to fine Don Larsen for breaking curfew*

"He went out to mail a letter."

> —CASEY STENGEL, *on what Larsen was doing out at 5 A.M.*

Curveballs

"He calls for the curveball so much because he figures since he can't hit it, nobody else can."

> —CASEY STENGEL, *on Mets catcher Chris Cannizzaro*

Cycle

"What would happen if I hit a triple? Ty Cobb would have been turning in his grave until he was upside down. Out of respect for Cobb, I didn't."

> —DARRIN FLETCHER, *a notoriously slow runner who needed only a triple for the cycle. (Ty Cobb was very fast and hit a lot of triples.)*

D

Babe Dahlgren

"He's a nice boy, but what would you get with nine Dahlgrens on your club?"

—JOE MCCARTHY, *on Babe Dahlgren*

Defense

"They should have called a welder."

—RICHIE ASHBURN, *on Dave Kingman, not a good fielder, having his glove repaired*

"As a pinch hitter, if you're one-for-four, you're doing your job. Defensively, they won't let you go one-for-four—I've tried it."

—ALAN BANNISTER

"Don't hit it to me."

> —JOSE CANSECO, *playing for the Red Sox, when asked how the Red Sox can improve their defense*

"I approach every fly ball like it's a knuckleball."

> —AL FERRARA, *former major-league outfielder*

"If you hit Polonia 100 fly balls, you could make a movie out of it—*Catch 22*."

> —DENNIS LAMP, *on the fielding ability of Luis Polonia*

"He has trouble with the thrown ball."

> —CHARLIE MANUEL, *his assessment of Sam Horn as a first baseman*

"In the outfield, fly balls are my only weakness."

> —CARMELO MARTINEZ

"The way he fielded ground balls, I knew he was going to wind up on the bench."

> —SAM MELE, *on college teammate Burton Roberts, who ended up as a judge*

"I hope Stuart doesn't think that means him."

> —DANNY MURTAUGH, *referring to first baseman Dick Stuart after the announcer said that anyone who interfered with a ball in play would be ejected from the stadium*

"Our fielders have to catch a lot of balls—or at least deflect them to someone who can."

> —DAN QUISENBERRY, *on a porous Royals defense*

"One night in Pittsburgh, 30,000 fans gave me a standing ovation when I caught a hot-dog wrapper on the fly."

> —DICK STUART

"As a first baseman, he's a good hitter."

> —JOE TORRE, *on Rusty Staub*

Designated Hitter

"I've changed my mind about it—instead of being bad, it stinks."

> —SPARKY ANDERSON, *on being a designated hitter*

"If I played all my career in the outfield, I'd have 500 home runs and 600 errors."

> —JOSE CANSECO, *on enjoying being a DH*

"I flush the toilet between innings to keep my wrists strong."

> —JOHN LOWENSTEIN, *on how he keeps toned between at bats as a DH*

"When you're a designated hitter, you have time to think about these things."

> —PAUL MOLITOR, *on being the third native of St. Paul to have a major accomplishment—3,000 hits—in the Metrodome. (Dave Winfield and Jack Morris were the other two.)*

"I'm not just a DH. I'm headed for the Hall of Fame."

> —RUBEN SIERRA

Devil Rays

"I don't want to wait that long for the next. Of course, I don't think I'll be allowed to wait that long."

> —LARRY ROTHSCHILD, *Devil Rays manager, on the Devil Rays having their first winning month in August of their second year*

Rob Dibble

"I tell him something and it goes in one ear and hits something hard and bounces back out."

> —DAVEY JOHNSON, *on Rob Dibble*

Diet

"You mix two jiggers of scotch and one jigger of Metrecal. So far I've lost five pounds and my driver's license."

> —ROCKY BRIDGES

Disappearing Act

"Every time I see him, he's not there."

> —YOGI BERRA, *when asked if he knew where Phil Rizzuto was during spring training*

"If you're such a good magician, why don't you make your next hitter disappear?"

> —DAN WARTHEN, *to Padres pitcher Dan Bochtler, who is a magician*

Divorce

"I need her like Custer needs Indians."

> —BO BELINSKY, *on breaking up with actress-wife Mamie Van Doren*

"I never realized how short a month is until I started paying alimony."

> —HARRY CARAY

Doctor, Doctor

"Oh, what's the matter with you now?"

> —YOGI BERRA, *after his wife said she was going to see Dr. Zhivago*

"I can't recall what medical school he graduated from. I'll have to check."

> —HARRY DALTON, *on Gary Sheffield resisting wrist surgery, thinking he would never be the same after the surgery*

"I don't know. It's like they were talking German to me."

> —DON ZIMMER, *when asked what his doctors told him after an MRI on his knee*

Dodgers

"In Los Angeles, finding celebrities to throw out the first pitch is not a problem. The hard part is finding a Dodger who can catch it."

> —JAY LENO

"The key to beating the Dodgers is to keep them from hugging each other too much."

> —GRAIG NETTLES, *on the Dodgers during the Lasorda era*

"The Dodgers are such a .500 club, they could probably split a three-game series."

> —VIN SCULLY

Dodgers Fans

"People in Southern California would leave early from sex."

> —SCOTT OSTLER

Dog-Eat-Dog

"I don't believe in doghouses, but if I did, this one could house Marmaduke."

> —JOHN BOLES, *Marlins manager, on Alex Gonzales not always hustling during games*

"The dog has not been suspended."

> —JIM BOWDEN, *on not being opposed to someone walking Reds owner Marge Schott's dog Schotzie on the field during Schott's suspension*

Doubleheader

"Does that mean the second game is off, too?"

> —JOHN HALE, *Mariners outfielder, after rain caused the cancellation of a doubleheader*

Drinking

"It depends on the length of the game."

> —KING KELLY, *when asked if he drank during games*

"I drink after wins. I drink after losses. I drink after rainouts."

> —BOB LEMON

"I'd like to help you, but you don't drink."

> —BOB LEMON, *to Don Kessinger, who had asked for advice on how to manage*

"Don't drink in the hotel bar. That's where I do my drinking."

> —CASEY STENGEL, *advice to players on how to avoid being caught drinking*

"I have never played drunk. Hungover, yes, but never drunk."

> —HACK WILSON

Dugout

"I told you we'd improve our bench."

> —JACK MCKEON, *on San Diego's dugout being renovated*

Ryne Duren

"Ryne Duren was a one-pitch pitcher. His one pitch was a wild warm-up."

—JIM BOUTON

Leo Durocher

"He has the ability to take a bad situation and make it immediately worse."

—BRANCH RICKEY, *on Durocher*

Lenny Dykstra

"There's so much tobacco juice all over the rug, you can get cancer by just standing out there. It's like a toxic waste dump."

—ANDY VAN SLYKE, *on seeing tobacco juice stains on the field from Phillies center fielder Lenny Dykstra*

Earful

"One hundred and ten thousand ears in this ballpark and he's got to hit my ear."

> —DON ZIMMER, *on being hit in the ear by a line drive during the '99 playoffs*

Education

"He seemed a little dense, but you know that's not unique with some ballplayers."

> —JOEL ARMSTRONG, *principal in a Florida elementary school, on an impersonator claiming to be a Florida Marlins player speaking at the school*

"I am not going to buy my kids an encyclopedia. Let them walk to school like I did."

> —YOGI BERRA, *when asked if he wanted to buy an encyclopedia for his kids*

"We're not dealing with who throws the first snowball. It's a little more complex now."

> —JOHN BOLES, *Marlins manager, on how he would use his teaching experience in managing the Marlins*

Ego

"I'm really proud of the fact that I'm as good a pitcher as he is, maybe better."

> —AL FITZMORRIS, *on Nolan Ryan*

"The more self-centered and egotistical a guy is, the better ballplayer he's going to be."

> —BILL LEE

England Swings

"Old Diz knows the King's English. And not only that, I also know the Queen is English."

—DIZZY DEAN, *on critics who make fun of his grammar*

Enron Field

"Do the walls move back?"

—ANDY ASHBY, *on the short fences in the Astros' new ballpark*

"Yeah, in runs they're putting on the board."

—JIM DESHAIES, *Astros announcer, when asked if the new stadium depicts anything he did during his pitching career*

Equipment Manager

"Putting a Rolex on me is like putting earrings on a pig."

> —BERNIE STOWE, *Reds equipment manager, on getting a Rolex watch for his retirement*

ERA

"Moderate is a Richter scale reading higher than the American League ERA. Strong is higher than the Tiger ERA."

> —DAVE AUST, *explaining the rating system for earthquakes—mild, moderate, and strong*

"It's not big if you look at it from the standpoint of the national debt."

> —BILL RIGNEY, *on the Twins' ERA*

Errors

"I've seen better hands on a clock."

> —MEL DURSLAG, *on Bill Russell's five errors during a doubleheader*

"The number played a very big part in my career because of E-6."

> —JIM FREGOSI, *on being a shortstop who wore the number 6*

"Soothe him? Soothe me."

> —JIM FREGOSI, *Blue Jays manager, when asked if he tried to soothe Todd Zeile after Zeile commited four errors in a game*

"You know you're in trouble when you say, 'Nice catch,' and it's the catcher you're talking about."

> —HANK GREENWALD, *on four passed balls in a game for catcher Mark Salas*

"They got two bases, and I got a urine test."

> —STEVE HOWE, *on throwing the ball over the third baseman during an appeal play*

"They're like vitamins—one a day."

> —ED SPRAGUE, *on his 11 errors early in the season*

"Errors are part of my image."

> —DICK STUART

"I look up in the stands and I see them miss balls too."

> —DEVON WHITE, *after being booed by fans for missing a fly ball*

ESPN

"That's the difference between a young player and an old player. The young player doesn't know how to get on SportsCenter."

> —MIKE GALLEGO, *on consistently diving for balls*

"What do I wanna do that for? They go out to 50 people, and I'm supposed to stop what I'm doing for them?"

—WHITEY HERZOG, *on refusing to be interviewed by ESPN during the network's first year*

Expansion Team

"Anyone who tells himself he can win a pennant with an expansion team is just spitting into a gale."

—ROY HARTSFIELD, *Blue Jays manager*

Experience

"Experience is a hard teacher, because she gives you the test first and the lesson afterwards."

—VERNON LAW

"The Pilgrims didn't have any experience when they first arrived here."

—DOUG RADER, *on being told he needed more experience before he would be hired as a manager*

Expos

"There ought to be a clause in our contract allowing us to veto a country."

—STEVE RENKO, *on being traded to the Expos*

"I can't concentrate against the Expos."

—JOHN ROCKER, *on his lack of respect for the Expos*

"It'll be great not to have to listen to two different national anthems."

—MITCH WEBSTER, *on being traded from the Expos*

Extra Innings

"We went the whole game without going to the bathroom."

—JACK LIETZ, *minor-league umpire, on what was most impressive about an eight-hour game between Rochester and Pawtucket*

"Forget about him. What about me?"

> —DAMIAN MILLER, *Diamondbacks catcher, after catching 92 straight innings, including a 16-inning game, when Manager Buck Showalter asked him how the pitcher was holding up*

Eye for an Eye

"Right now I can't find my glasses without my glasses."

> —ART HOWE, *on why he needed laser eye surgery*

"I wore my right contact on my left eye and my left contact on my right eye. When I thought a pitch was down and in, it was really up and away. And when I thought a pitch was up and away, it was really down and in."

> —JUNIOR ORTIZ, *explaining why he struck out twice in a game and went hitless*

F

Facial Hair

"Who knows? It might have come in gray."

> —BRETT BUTLER, *on getting older and deciding against growing a beard*

"I still have it. I just keep it shaved."

> —GARY GAETTI, *when asked what had become of his mustache*

Family

"Playing for Yogi is like playing for your father. Playing for Billy [Martin] is like playing for your father-in-law."

> —DON BAYLOR

"Billy Almon has all of his inlaws and outlaws here this afternoon."

> —JERRY COLEMAN

"I looked at his press list and asked him if it was the cast from *Deliverance*."

> —TIM FLANNERY, *after John Kruk invited 50 family members to come to a game*

"They shouldn't throw at me. I'm the father of five or six kids."

> —TITO FUENTES, *on a brush-back pitch*

"If I had a daughter and she came home with Tom or Larry, I'd be happy. But if she came home with me or Joe, I'd kill her."

> —JOHN KRUK, *on his three brothers*

"I could use a stronger word, and I will—I find it deplorable."

> —BOWIE KUHN, *on wife swapping between Yankees teammates Fritz Peterson and Mike Kekich*

"If I worried about my own children as much as I worry about these kids, I'd get a Father of the Year award."

—LOU PINIELLA, *on keeping Norm Charlton and Rob Dibble happy early in their careers*

"When I played baseball, I got death threats all the time—from my mother."

—BOB UECKER

"I signed with the Milwaukee Braves for $3,000. That bothered my dad at the time, because he didn't have that kind of dough to pay out. But eventually he scraped it up."

—BOB UECKER

Fancy Titles

"I think that means I'm the general manager."

—JIM FREY, *on being named VP of Operations with the Cubs*

Fans

"They're jealous. When we go to McDonald's or Burger King, we don't yell at them if our burgers aren't cooked right."

> —CARLOS CASTILLO, *White Sox pitcher, on being booed by fans*

"We like to educate our fans."

> —BOBBY VALENTINE, *on getting into an argument with an unruly fan*

"Out in the stands, drinking beer and yelling, 'Get Yoshii in there.' "

> —MASATO YOSHII, *asked where he would be if he was not on the Mets' playoff roster*

Fastball

"I tried to throw cheese [fastball], but it wasn't a sharp cheddar. It was more like a soft Brie."

> —LARRY ANDERSEN, *after an injury*

"My change-up."

> —BOB FELLER, *on Rob Nen's 102-mph fastball*

Fenway Park

"I don't know. I've never pitched in a phone booth before."

> —GENE CONLEY, *when asked how he would feel about pitching in Fenway Park*

"Do they leave it there during the game?"

> —BILL LEE, *upon seeing the Green Monster for the first time*

Fight Night

"I don't throw the first punch. I throw the second four."

> —BILLY MARTIN

"Baseball players are the worst fighters I've seen in my entire life. The guy chasing the mound is thinking, 'What the hell do I do now that I'm here?'"

—BILL RIGNEY

Fines

"The cops picked me up on a street at 3 A.M. and fined me $500 for being drunk and $100 for being with the Phillies."

—BOB UECKER

Charlie Finley

"I knew Alvin Dark was a religious man, but he's worshiping the wrong god, Charlie Finley."

—VIDA BLUE

"A woman asked me the other day if there's any truth to the rumor that Charlie Finley is out to get me. I said, 'Honey, that ain't no rumor.'"

—BOWIE KUHN

"Charlie Finley is a self-made man who worships his creator."

> —JIM MURRAY

"I'll last a lot longer managing here than I would in Oakland for Charlie Finley."

> —JOHNNY VANDER MEER, *on managing an old-timers' team during spring training*

Fireman

"It can be life or death in the fire service, and it definitely felt like life or death on the ballfield."

> —ALLAN ANDERSON, *on being a fireman and a professional baseball player*

Firing Line

"You never ask why you've been fired, because if you do, they're likely to tell you."

> —JERRY COLEMAN

"If you don't win, you're going to be fired. If you do win, you're only putting off the day you're going to be fired."

—LEO DUROCHER

"If they fire me, I'll be the highest-paid fisherman in the country."

—WHITEY HERZOG

"Patience is great, but patience can get you fired."

—WHITEY HERZOG, *when asked if he would be patient with a player in a slump*

"Better Billy Martin than Dick Howser."

—DICK HOWSER, *on hearing that Billy Martin had just been rehired for a fourth term as Yankees manager*

"He was like a college professor. I thought he had tenure."

—MIKE MACFARLANE, *on Bobby Valentine being fired after many years as the Rangers manager*

"Joe tried to treat the players like men, but it's well known that most ballplayers are a bunch of asses."

>—BILL MADLOCK, *on Joe Altobelli's firing as manager of the Giants*

"He may still be available."

>—MICKEY MANTLE, *on Billy Martin not being available for a golf tournament because he had just been hired as the A's manager*

"All I know is, I pass people on the street these days, and they don't know whether to say hello or to say good-bye."

>—BILLY MARTIN, *during one of his incarnations as a Yankees manager*

"I can usually tell you by the number of writers—there aren't enough here yet."

>—GENE MICHAEL, *after he was asked if he was being fired*

"I think they recycle more managers than cars."

>—BILLY NORTH

"If you're the Yankees manager with the team on a road trip, you'd be wise not to send out your laundry."

    —PHIL RIZZUTO

"A manager is like a fellow swimming in the ocean with a cut on his arm. Sooner or later, the sharks are going to get him."

    —EDDIE STANKY

"It's an outright lie that I fired an office girl over a tuna fish sandwich. I'm almost certain it was peanut butter and jelly."

    —GEORGE STEINBRENNER

Fly Ball

"I never knew what Joe DiMaggio looked like until I roomed with him. All I ever saw was the back of his uniform after I threw a pitch."

    —LEFTY GOMEZ

"Somebody told me after the game that the shortest distance between two points is a straight line. But I was poor in geometry. I always thought it was an isosceles triangle."

> —ANDY VAN SLYKE, *after he ran the wrong way on a fly ball and the hitter ended up with an inside-the-park home run*

Food for Thought

"It's so bad, the people who serve it won't eat it."

> —JACK BUCK, *on the food in Atlanta*

"Do you know what I miss most about baseball? The pine tar, the resin, the grass, the dirt—and that's just in the hot dog."

> —DAVID LETTERMAN, *on a baseball strike*

"The best way to avoid ballplayers is to go to a good restaurant."

> —TIM MCCARVER

"I used to be the toast of Toronto. Now I'm the jelly."

> —LLOYD MOSEBY, *on seeing his star drop*

"No, thanks—I don't drink."

> —JEFF STONE, *when asked if he wanted shrimp cocktail*

"Outrageous, really outrageous. I'm not sure I won't eat before I come to the game."

> —TED TURNER, *on the price of the food at Fulton County Stadium*

Foul Balls

"I talked to the ball a lot of times in my career. I yelled, 'Go foul, go foul.'"

> —LEFTY GOMEZ

Ford Frick

"There was a vacancy when I left, and the owners decided to continue with it."

—HAPPY CHANDLER, *on Ford Frick being hired as commissioner after Chandler stepped down*

"He slept longer while in office than Rip Van Winkle."

—HAPPY CHANDLER, *on Frick*

Future

"The future ain't what it used to be."

—YOGI BERRA

"Ten million years from now, when the sun burns out and the earth is just a frozen iceberg hurtling through space, nobody's going to care whether or not I got this guy out."

—TUG MCGRAW

G

Gamblin' Man

"I see we're advertising casinos now. Gambling must be OK. Bud Selig is going to call me any day now."

—PETE ROSE, *about a casino billboard in the Phillies' spring training facility*

Lou Gehrig

"I took the two most expensive aspirins in history."

—WALLY PIPP, *on being replaced in the Yankees' lineup by Gehrig, who did not miss a game for over a decade*

Giants

"I don't think they could hit more home runs if you told them what was coming."

—DUSTY BAKER, *on the opposing teams to whom the Giants gave up 24 home runs in a seven-game stretch*

"I don't mind turning 50. It's just at the beginning of the season I was 43."

—HANK GREENWALD, *on a tough year for the Giants*

Gold Gloves

"The only way I'm going to win a Gold Glove is with a can of spray paint."

—REGGIE JACKSON

Golf Game

"It took me 17 years to get 3,000 hits. I did it in one afternoon on the golf course."

—HANK AARON

"I was three over—one over a house, one over a patio, and one over a swimming pool."

—GEORGE BRETT

"When I hit a ball, I want someone else to go chase it."

—ROGERS HORNSBY, *on why he didn't play golf*

"I tell myself that Jack Nicklaus probably has a lousy curveball."

—BOB WALK, *Pirates pitcher, on being a lousy golfer*

Gopher Ball

"It was a cross between a screwball and a change-up.
It was a screw-up."

> —BOB PATTERSON, *on a pitch he threw to Barry Larkin, who hit it for a home run*

Rich Gossage

"The Goose should do more pitching and less
quacking."

> —GEORGE STEINBRENNER, *after Gossage voiced his concerns about the Yankees*

Grade School

"I didn't do so great in the first grade either."

> —DIZZY DEAN, *on dropping out of school after second grade*

Grammar

"Some people who don't say ain't, ain't eating."

—DIZZY DEAN, *on the criticism of his grammar*

Greed

"I think greed is a terrible thing—unless you're in on the ground floor."

—YOGI BERRA

Dallas Green

"You found out where you stood only if you could afford to buy all the newspapers the next day."

—BOB BOONE, *on having Dallas Green as a manager*

"He thinks he invented the game."

—DON ZIMMER, *on Green*

H

Hail to the Chief

"He sat right where I usually sit. I didn't have the heart to say, 'Move over.' "

> —JOE ALTOBELLI, *on Ronald Reagan sitting in Altobelli's seat in the Orioles' clubhouse on opening day*

"Get the presidents out of the game. If I come up and Joe Carter's out there, I'll give up."

> —ANDY VAN SLYKE, *after being robbed of home runs by Otis Nixon and Claudell Washington*

Hairstyle

"I call it the Watergate. I cover up everything I can."

—JOE TORRE, *on his hairstyle*

Hall of Fame

"I might be the only one to be rejected in three categories."

—RICHIE ASHBURN, *prior to his induction into the Hall of Fame, on being a player, broadcaster, and newspaper columnist*

"That's amazing. I'm in the Hall of Fame and Bill Mazeroski isn't."

—CHARLIE FEENEY, *sportswriter from Pittsburgh, inducted into the baseball writers' wing*

"Daryl Strawberry has been voted to the Hall of Fame five years in a row."

—RALPH KINER

"It seems strange to me that some fellows have passed me on the ballot without any of us getting any more hits."

> —JOHNNY MIZE, *on Hall of Fame voting*

"In the American League, all called strikes are sent to the Hall of Fame."

> —KEITH OLBERMANN, *after Tigers pitcher Brian Moehler threw the first pitch at Comerica Park for a called strike and the game was stopped to retrieve the ball for Cooperstown*

"When I asked the baseball writers why they hadn't elected me to the Hall of Fame, they told me they thought I was still playing."

> —BOB UECKER

Height Report

"The bases were too high."

> —JOHN CANGELOSI, *5′9″, after tripping over a base*

Rickey Henderson

"Has he ever been here the first day? You have to say Rickey's consistent. That's what you want in a ballplayer, consistency."

—DON MATTINGLY, *on Rickey Henderson consistently showing up late for spring training*

Orlando Hernandez

"He's a very lucky man. He escapes the dictatorial reign of a ruthless tyrant and ends up working for George Steinbrenner."

—DAVID LETTERMAN, *on El Duque*

Whitey Herzog

"They call him the rat because he's always jumping off sinking ships."

—KEITH HERNANDEZ, *on Whitey Herzog, nicknamed "the White Rat"*

High School

"I only had a high school education, and believe me, I had to cheat to get that."

—SPARKY ANDERSON

"In high school, I took a little English, some science, and some hubcaps and some wheel covers."

—GATES BROWN

"One reporter asked me about the chemistry on this club. I told him I didn't even pass biology in high school."

—JIM FREY, *as the Cubs manager*

"We were the gold dust twins. He got the gold and I got the dust."

—PHIL GAGLIANO, *a career utility player and high school teammate of Tim McCarver*

"You know what they put by my picture in the 11th-grade yearbook? It was 'He'll get a gold watch for his service.'"

—MIKE KILKENNY, *on dropping out of high school*

Hip Hop

"Has anybody ever satisfactorily explained why the bad
hop is always the last one?"

—HANK GREENWALD

Hit and Run

"He got hit so hard, I had to get all the married men
off the field."

—WHITEY HERZOG, *on Ken Dayley*

"I know, Jim, but the outfielders are."

—JEFF TORBORG, *on taking the ball away from
pitcher Jim Kern even though Kern said he
wasn't tired*

Hit by Pitch

"The strike zone is little, people are big."

—PEDRO MARTINEZ, *early in his career, on
knocking down hitters*

"He had great command of his pitches. He hit them both in the same spot."

> —JEFF TORBORG, *after pitcher Jeff Innis hit Mariano Duncan and Wes Chamberlain on virtually the same spot on their bodies*

Sterling Hitchcock

"I don't even know who Sterling Hitchcock is. I thought he was Alfred's kid. Him throwing at me wasn't too cool."

> —DEION SANDERS, *on Sterling Hitchcock throwing at him*

Hitters

"What do you want me to do? Let those sons of bitches stand up there and think on my time?"

> —GROVER CLEVELAND ALEXANDER, *on throwing successive pitches quickly*

"I hate all hitters. I start a game mad and stay that
way until it's over."

—DON DRYSDALE

Hitters Pitching

"He should have to go back to 2,998."

—JEFF CONINE, *on Wade Boggs, who had 3,001
hits at the time, being used to pitch in a
blowout game in which he gave up three hits*

Hollywood

"Hollywood sucks. I sat around for hours on end with
nothing to do."

—JOHN KRUK, *on his acting debut in the movie*
The Fan

Home Plate

"If they had a picture of Tyra Banks on the plate, I might kiss it. Otherwise, I'm not going near that filthy thing."

—DOUG GLANVILLE, *when asked if he could ever kiss home plate the way Wade Boggs did after getting his 3,000th hit*

Home Runs

"Home run? I never even hit the wall."

—SPARKY ANDERSON, *when asked if any of his 104 hits were home runs*

"It's pretty hard when the family asks for passes to the game and want to sit in the left-field bleachers."

—BERT BLYLEVEN, *on setting the record for giving up the most home runs in a season*

"Every once in a while the Good Lord sends me down a little sunshine—even if we were playing under a roof."

> —JIM EISENREICH, *on hitting his first two home runs of the season in June at the Astrodome*

"I wanted to go into my home-run trot, but I realized I didn't have one."

> —JIM ESSIAN, *on his first home run in over 100 games*

"He should have bought tickets when I was pitching."

> —CHUCK FINLEY, *on Charlie Sheen buying all the tickets in the left-field stands in Anaheim so he could be guaranteed to catch a home-run ball. But no one hit a ball out there.*

"That's not baseball. That's T-ball."

> —KEN GRIFFEY SR., *on baseball's emphasis on home runs*

"We're not even going to catch Roger Maris."

> —WHITEY HERZOG, *on a weak-hitting Cardinals team*

"Five."

> —ALEX JOHNSON, *when asked to explain the difference in power from hitting two home runs in a year to hitting seven early in the next season*

"What's one home run? If you hit one, they are going to want you to hit two."

> —MICK KELLEHER, *after hitting a rare home run*

"I'm mad at him for deciding to play one more season. I threw his last home run and thought I'd be remembered forever. Now I have to throw him another."

> —BILL LEE, *on giving up Hank Aaron's 745th home run, thinking it was Aaron's last season. Aaron came back for one more year.*

"I'd have taken it even if it bounced off his head and went out."

> —SCOTT LIVINGSTONE, *on hitting a rare home run that bounced off the outfielder's glove*

"Please tell me he had at least one in Little League."

> —DONN PALL, *after giving up Felix Fermin's first major-league home run*

"Reggie Jackson hit one off me in Kansas City that's still burrowing it's way to St. Louis."

—DAN QUISENBERRY

Horsing Around

"I treat my horses better than the owners treat us."

—DICK ALLEN, *horse owner*

"I like my horses better because they can't talk to sportswriters."

—GEORGE STEINBRENNER, *comparing his horses to the players on the Yankees*

Houston

"This is the only town where women wear insect repellent instead of perfume."

—RICHIE ASHBURN, *on Houston*

I

Illness

"Baseball and malaria keep coming back."

—GENE MAUCH

Indians

"Our own."

—PETER BAVASI, *Indians general manager, on the team he fears the most in baseball*

"With the A's, we depended on pitching and speed to win. With the Giants, we depended upon pitching and power to win. With the Indians, we depended upon an act of God."

—ALVIN DARK, *on his managerial experiences*

"The first thing they do in Cleveland if you have talent is trade you for three guys who don't."

—JIM KERN

"I always liked working Indians games, because they were usually out of the pennant race by the end of April, and there was never too much pressure on the umpires."

—RON LUCIANO

"When you play on a team like Cleveland, what you are trying to do is impress other general managers. What you are trying to say is, 'Look at me, I'm a good player. Make a deal for me.'"

—GRAIG NETTLES, *on the Indians in the late '70s*

"In Cleveland, pennant fever usually ends up being a 48-hour virus."

—FRANK ROBINSON

"The only good thing about playing in Cleveland is that you don't have to make road trips there."

—RICHIE SCHEINBLUM

Injuries

"Does that mean I can have a simulated beer when I get back to the clubhouse?"

> —LARRY ANDERSEN, *on pitching two simulated innings after coming off the disabled list*

"I was thinking about making a comeback until I pulled a muscle vacuuming."

> —JOHNNY BENCH, *on talks of his comeback*

"If I were a racehorse, I would be disqualified."

> —JOHNNY BENCH, *on all the medication he was taking for his injuries*

"Back then, if you had a sore arm, the only people concerned were you and your wife. Now it's you, your wife, your agent, your investment counselor, your stockbroker, and your publisher."

> —JIM BOUTON

"Bruce Benedict may not be hurt as much as he really is."

> —JERRY COLEMAN

"Ricky's an important guy, but it's not like Bagwell's hurt."

> —LARRY DIERKER, *Astros manager, on Ricky Gutierrez's broken thumb*

"If World War III breaks out, we'll win the pennant by 20 games, because none of our guys could pass the physical."

> —WHITEY HERZOG, *on rampant injuries on the Cardinals team*

"When I broke in, we had one trainer who carried a bottle of rubbing alcohol and by the seventh inning he had drunk it all."

> —TOMMY LASORDA, *on the assortment of injuries of today's players*

"We've had more MRIs than RBIs."

> —JACK MCKEON, *on injuries to the Reds*

"The only thing ice is good for is Scotch."

> —TERRY MULHOLLAND, *after he was told to rest his injured arm and put ice on it*

"The way our luck has been lately, our fellas have been getting hurt on their days off."

> —CASEY STENGEL

"I never had any quads when I played."

> —DICK WILLIAMS, *on Spike Owen missing a game because of an injured quad*

"We had a lot of guys hurt, but all we can do is put our best foot forward and try not to sprain it."

> —KEVIN YOUNG, *on the Pirates having 12 players injured*

Investments

"Are you crazy? I was investing in Ferraris."

> —JOSE CANSECO, *who created his own financial group, when asked if he ever imagined doing that early in his career*

IQ Test

"The Good Lord was good to me. He gave me a strong body, a good right arm, and a weak mind."

> —DIZZY DEAN

"The kid is the greatest proof of reincarnation. Nobody could get that stupid in one lifetime."

> —JOE MCCARTHY, *on a player thrown out trying to steal home with one out*

"Tell a ballplayer something a thousand times, then tell him again, because that might be the time he'll understand something."

> —PAUL RICHARDS

"Out of what—a thousand?"

—MICKEY RIVERS, *on Reggie Jackson's claim of
a 160 IQ*

"He is the first player to make the major leagues with
one brain cell."

—ROY SMALLEY, *on Mickey Hatcher*

"Open up a ballplayer's head and you know what you'd
find? A lot of little broads and a jazz band."

—MAYO SMITH

"You should forget about these big words. You can't
get 'em out in the library."

—CASEY STENGEL, *to Mets pitcher Jay Hook,
who had a genius IQ*

Hideki Irabu

"That's the difference between this year and last year. This year he has a funny interpreter."

—DEREK JETER, *on Irabu laughing with Yankee teammates more during his second year than during his first*

Mike Ivie

"If anybody wants him, they can have him."

—FRANK ROBINSON, *on Mike Ivie demanding to be traded*

J

Danny Jackson

"Every fifth day, he'd destroy a TV or phone. That's why we called him Jason."

> —MARK GRACE, *on the temper of teammate and pitcher Danny Jackson*

Reggie Jackson

"The only thing Reggie can do better than me on the field is talk."

> —ROD CAREW

"It's not that Reggie is a bad outfielder. He just has trouble judging the ball and picking it up."

> —BILLY MARTIN

"The only thing missing is there's no mustard in it."

> —MICKEY RIVERS, *on the Reggie! candy bar*

Japan

"The motto of the team I played for was 'win or else.' I didn't know what the 'else' meant—I never wanted to learn."

> —CHUCK CARY, *on playing in Japan*

"Baseball is very different in Japan. For example, if you're at third base, before coming home, you have to take off your shoes."

> —BILL MAHER

"I would for the right amount of sushi."

> —ANDY VAN SLYKE, *when asked if he would ever play in Japan*

Jobs

"Probably shoveling manure on a farm."

> —TOM KELLY, *on what he would be doing if he didn't play baseball*

"I'm a vice president in charge of sports marketing. That means I play golf and go to cocktail parties. I'm pretty good at my job."

> —MICKEY MANTLE

"It gets more exciting every year, but I wish they'd give me something to do."

> —STAN MUSIAL, *on being a VP with the Cardinals*

Darrell Johnson

"I did not call Johnson an idiot. Someone else did, and I just agreed."

> —JIM PALMER, *denying that he called Darrell Johnson an idiot for not playing Palmer in an All-Star Game*

Doug Jones

"He throws that slop when he's behind in the count, and he throws that slop when he's ahead in the count. You can't hit it."

—JOHN KRUK, *on the slow pitches of Doug Jones*

Michael Jordan

"The game needs someone like Michael Jordan to liven it up. All these players are so mediocre. Hit .230 and you make $3 million."

—CHARLES BARKLEY, *on Michael Jordan playing baseball*

"He's not a natural hitter. He couldn't hit a curveball with an ironing board."

—BOB FELLER, *on Michael Jordan*

K

Kingdome

"In this ballpark, I feel that when you're walking to the plate, you're in scoring position."

—DON BAYLOR, *on the Kingdome*

Knuckleball

"A curveball that doesn't give a damn."

—JIMMY CANNON, *describing a knuckleball*

"A stadium with the lights out."

—CHARLIE HOUGH, *knuckleball pitcher, on the best situation for a knuckleball pitcher*

"I'd rather have my legs cut off than do that all day. You just hope it hits your bat in a good spot."

> —JOHN KRUK, *on hitting the knuckleball*

"He can embarrass the batter on one pitch and the catcher on the next pitch."

> —RON TINGLEY, *on catching for knuckleball pitcher Charlie Hough*

"The way to catch a knuckleball is to wait until the ball stops rolling and then pick it up."

> —BOB UECKER

"I'd have a better chance of catching flies with chopsticks."

> —ANDY VAN SLYKE, *on hitting knucklers*

"It's not something you can practice. It's like practicing javelin catching."

> —ANDY VAN SLYKE, *on how to prepare to hit off Charlie Hough*

Sandy Koufax

"The day I got a hit off Koufax was when he knew it
 was all over."

>—SPARKY ANDERSON

John Kruk

"John Kruk is the luckiest man in baseball. He has not
 only his number on the back of his uniform, but his
 picture too."

>—GREG BOOKER, *Padres pitching coach, on
> John Kruk wearing the number 8, which is
> shaped like Kruk's body*

"Watching him out there is like watching 'Unsolved
 Mysteries.'"

>—JOE GARAGIOLA, *describing the fielding of
> John Kruk*

"He's overweight, out of shape, and built like a plumber. You look at him and wait for stuff to start falling off."

> —MITCH WILLIAMS, *on Kruk*

Bowie Kuhn

"I have often called him the village idiot. I apologize to all the village idiots of America. He's the nation's idiot."

> —CHARLIE FINLEY, *on Bowie Kuhn*

"If Bowie Kuhn doesn't stop, he'll lead us into World War III."

> —WHITEY HERZOG, *on the lack of direction displayed by Bowie Kuhn*

Duane Kuiper

"Duane's game reminds me of a lot of the bars I go to—all singles and no action."

—DOUG DIEKEN, *football pro, on the hitting of Duane Kuiper*

L

Labor

"I was accused of being soft on labor, which is like
being accused of being soft on Communism in the
'50s."

—FAY VINCENT

Language Barrier

"How do you say *adios* in Spanish?"

—CLAY CARROL

Don Larsen

"The only thing he fears is sleep."

—JIMMY DYKES, on the lifestyle of Don Larsen

Tommy Lasorda

"Tommy's the only manager in the major leagues who uses a fork for a letter opener."

—RICK MONDAY, on Lasorda's penchant for eating

Last Place

"I'd rather be in a prison cell with Mike Tyson and let him beat my butt all day long than go through that again."

—JOHN KRUK, on the Phillies finishing last in '92

Law and Order

"I did pass the bar. But as some might say, I haven't passed one since."

> —MEL ALLEN, *legendary Yankees announcer, on passing the bar exam*

"I'd rather ride the buses while managing in Triple-A than be a lawyer."

> —TONY LARUSSA, *on passing the bar exam but never actually practicing law*

"We're going to charge them double, bill them by the third of an inning, and generally berate them."

> —MIKE VEECK, *VP of marketing for the Devil Rays, on having a lawyers appreciation night*

Leaders

"One percent of ballplayers are leaders of men. The other 99 percent are followers or worse."

> —JOHN MCGRAW

League Leaders

"You've got to lead the league in something."

> —DALE MOHORCIC, *on leading the league in balks after balking twice in the first two games of the year*

Literary Life

"Before he writes a book, he's got to read one."

> —DALLAS GREEN, *on Rickey Henderson threatening to write a tell-all book about the Yankees*

"Sparky is the only guy I know who has written more books than he has read."

> —ERNIE HARWELL, *on Sparky Anderson's autobiography*

"One of them had me dead already."

> —MARK KOENIG, *a member of the '27 Yankees team, when asked if he had any opinion about the books written about the '27 Yankees*

"I didn't put stuff like that in my book. Of course, I didn't sell many books."

> —LOU PINIELLA, *comparing his book to Dave Winfield's tell-all book*

Little League

"My wife is probably going to organize a Little League for me just to get me out of the house."

> —TERRY COLLINS, *on what he would do after being fired*

"It exists for parents who are trying vicariously to recover an ability of their own that never really existed."

> —BILL VEECK, *on Little League*

Locker Room

"When I was in baseball and you went into the clubhouse, you didn't see ballplayers with curling irons."

> —RED BARBER

Long Innings

"Yeah, but it was in this inning."

> —BOB UECKER'S HIGH SCHOOL MANAGER, *after Uecker, who was pitching, told the manager he should stay in the game because he could get the batter out, having already struck him out once*

Looks Could Kill

"So I'm ugly. I never saw anybody hit with his face."

> —YOGI BERRA

Losing

"One of two things is happening. Either Miller is out there somewhere, or we've been very bad."

> —SPARKY ANDERSON, *on the Tigers' eight-game losing streak that stopped Anderson from tying Miller Huggins for 14th on the all-time manager win list*

"At this rate, in 18 years I'll be a 20-game winner."

> —MATT BEECH, *Phillies pitcher, on going more than a year between wins while losing 11 in a row*

"How can a guy win a game if you don't give him any runs?"

> —BO BELINSKY, *on losing a game 15–0*

"If a tie is like kissing your sister, losing is like kissing your grandmother with her teeth out."

> —GEORGE BRETT

"I managed a team that was so bad, we considered a 2–0 count on the batter a rally."

> —RICH DONNELLY

"Show me a good loser in professional sports, and I'll show you an idiot."

> —LEO DUROCHER

"I learned a lot, but I don't want to learn it again."

> —MATT KEOUGH, *on what he learned during 18 losses in a row*

"From Cy Young to sayonara in one year."

> —GRAIG NETTLES, *on Sparky Lyle winning the Cy Young Award, then being traded the following year*

"We were as flat tonight as people used to think the earth was."

> —DANNY OZARK, *on a bad Phillies loss*

Connie Mack

"I don't know. I never paid any attention to him."

—LEFTY GROVE, *on what Connie Mack was like as a manager*

Malaprops and Fractured Syntax

"Listen up, because I've got nothing to say and I'm only going to say it once."

—YOGI BERRA

"Yeah, only in America can a thing like that happen."

> —YOGI BERRA, *on a Jewish mayor being elected in Dublin, Ireland*

"You should always go to other people's funerals. Otherwise, they won't come to yours."

> —YOGI BERRA

"We made too many wrong mistakes."

> —YOGI BERRA, *after the Yankees lost the '60 World Series*

"A home opener is always exciting, no matter if it's at home or on the road."

> —YOGI BERRA

"Tony Perez is a big clog in their machine."

> —YOGI BERRA, *on Tony Perez and the Big Red Machine*

"Gaylord Perry and Willie McCovey should know each other like a book. They've been ex-teammates for years now."

> —JERRY COLEMAN

"Ron Guidry is not very big, maybe 140 pounds, but he has an arm like a lion."

> —JERRY COLEMAN

"It looks like the all-star balloting is about over, especially in the National and American League."

> —JERRY COLEMAN, *on all-star voting*

"I've made a couple of mistakes I'd like to do over."

> —JERRY COLEMAN

"Next up is Fernando Gonzales, who is not playing tonight."

> —JERRY COLEMAN

"Rick Folkers is throwing up in the bullpen."

> —JERRY COLEMAN

"Jesus Alou is in the on-deck circus."

> —JERRY COLEMAN

"If you asked what the Achilles tendon of the team is, it would be the pitching."

> —JERRY COLEMAN

"The Phillies beat the Cubs today in a doubleheader.
That puts another keg in the Cubs' coffin."

> —JERRY COLEMAN

"Graig Nettles leaps up to make one of those diving
stops only he can make."

> —JERRY COLEMAN

"I must have had ambrosia."

> —JIM GANTNER, *on missing a radio show
> appearance*

"Jose Canseco leads off the third inning with a grand
slam."

> —JOHN GORDON, *Twins announcer*

"It's permanent for now."

> —ROBERTO KELLY, *when asked if he was
> officially changing his name to Bobby*

"Rookie Wilson was a candidate for Mookie of the
Year."

> —RALPH KINER, *on Mookie Wilson*

"All of his saves have come in relief appearances."

—RALPH KINER

"Don Bordello's coming up to the plate."

—RALPH KINER, *on Dann Bilardello*

"Kevin McReynolds stops at third, and he scores."

—RALPH KINER

"Scott Sanderson was traded from Montreal on Pearl Harbor Day, June 7, 1983."

—RALPH KINER

"It's like a foreign city."

—MARK LANGSTON, *when asked if he had a problem playing in Montreal*

"I was only going about three-fourths to 75 percent."

—MIKE LIEBERTHAL

"I will perish this trophy forever."

—JOHNNY LOGAN

"I'll have pie à la mode with ice cream."

> —JOHNNY LOGAN

"What were they supposed to be taking? Was it those illegal amphibians?"

> —FRANK LUCCHESI, *on a drug case involving some Phillies*

"No longer than that. Maybe a month and a half."

> —JUNIOR ORTIZ, *when asked if an injury would keep him out for six weeks*

"Even Napoleon had his Watergate."

> —DANNY OZARK

"My jobs are to hit .300, score 100 runs, and stay injury prone."

> —MICKEY RIVERS

"Me and George and Billy are two of a kind."

> —MICKEY RIVERS, *on George Steinbrenner, Billy Martin, and himself*

"My elbow feels better after they gave me a chromosome shot."

> —GARY SERUM

"There's a woman protecting herself from the sun with a carousel."

> —MIKE SHANNON

"Their starting pitching could be a strong weakness."

> —KEVIN SLATEN, *Cardinals announcer*

"I was a victim of circumcision."

> —PETE VUKOVICH, *Pirates pitching coach, on being thrown out of a game*

"It was a real cliff dweller."

> —WES WESTRUM, *on a close game*

"Winfield robbed Armas of at least a home run."

> —BILL WHITE, *on a great catch made by Dave Winfield*

"Ninety percent of the game is half mental."

> —JIM WOHLFORD

"He hit it a lot further than it went."

—CURT YOUNG, *on a Rickey Henderson home run*

"It could just as easily have gone the other way."

—DON ZIMMER, *on a Cubs 4–4 road trip*

Managing

"I'm happy for him. That is, if you think being a big-league manager is a good thing to have happen to you."

—WALT ALSTON, *on Gil Hodges taking his first major-league managerial job*

"A baseball manager is a necessary evil."

—SPARKY ANDERSON

"You don't have to be a Harvard professor to manage baseball. In fact, I think you're better off having an IQ like mine."

—SPARKY ANDERSON

"There are three things that every man thinks he can do better than everybody else: build a fire, run a motel, and manage a baseball team."

—ROCKY BRIDGES

"I was no genius. If you don't have the players, you can't win."

—BUCKY HARRIS

"Most of the managers were lifetime .220 hitters. For years, pitchers have been getting those guys out 75 percent of the time. That's why they don't like us."

—BILL LEE

"Most pitchers are too smart to manage."

—JIM PALMER

"My feeling is that when you're managing a baseball team, you have to pick the right people to play and then pray a lot."

—ROBIN ROBERTS

"I had no trouble communicating. The players just didn't like what I had to say."

—FRANK ROBINSON

"Managing is getting paid for home runs that someone else hits."

—CASEY STENGEL

"What the heck is it but telling the umpire who's gonna play and then watching them play?"

—CASEY STENGEL, *on managing*

"I've never been wrong yet. They just didn't execute what I wanted them to do."

—CHUCK TANNER

Marlins

"The Marlins are going down as the king of dismantlers. I mean, ours was dismantling at its finest—record breaking."

—JOHN BOLES, *Marlins manager, when asked to compare the dismantling of the Padres to that of the Marlins*

"People look at us like we are the Bad News Bears."

> —GARY SHEFFIELD, *on the Marlins going from winning the World Series to dismantling the team*

Marriage

"I've had marriages that didn't last that long."

> —SKIP CARAY, *on announcing an 11-inning-long Braves game*

"No, I wanted to dedicate it to Bill Klem, the greatest umpire who ever lived. What the hell does my wife know about baseball?"

> —JOCKO CONLAN, *Hall of Fame umpire, when asked if he would dedicate his autobiography to his wife*

"The honeymoon is over."

> —DAVE DOMBROWSKI, *Marlins GM, on the winter meetings starting just as his honeymoon was ending*

"It keeps my marriage intact. I don't know what would happen if I was home all the time."

> —RICH GOSSAGE, *on the major advantage of his 20-year career*

Mike Marshall

"He likes to complain about not playing, which is what he does best."

> —PAT GILLICK, *on outfielder Mike Marshall demanding a trade*

Billy Martin

"Billy could never say anything that smart."

> —CAL GRIFFITH, *upon hearing that Billy Martin said of Reggie Jackson and George Steinbrenner, "One's a born liar, the other's convicted."*

"When he reaches for a bar tab, his arm shrinks six inches."

> —TOMMY LASORDA, *on Billy Martin*

"Some people have a chip on their shoulders. Billy has a whole lumberyard."

> —JIM MURRAY, *on Martin*

Gene Mauch

"I really like him, but what has he ever won?"

> —LEO DUROCHER, *on Gene Mauch*

Mark McGwire

"I'm glad. That leaves three less walks I have to watch."

> —JIM BOWDEN, *Reds GM, on McGwire sitting out a game because of an injury*

"If it doesn't work out well, Mark took a shot in the National League, and we took a shot."

> —TONY LARUSSA, *on a slow start by McGwire after McGwire was traded to the National League*

Media

"I wish they'd shut the gates and let us play ball with no press and no fans."

> —DICK ALLEN

"What, did Boris Yeltsin cancel?"

> —BRADY ANDERSON, *on having a great year and being asked to be interviewed by* "Meet the Press"

"A day without newspapers is like walking around without your pants on."

> —JERRY COLEMAN

"They don't ask any dumber questions than the guys do."

> —JIM FREGOSI, *on how he feels about female reporters*

"Sometimes they write what I say and not what I mean."

> —PEDRO GUERRERO

"I try to have respect for people in general, whether it's baseball players or lowlifes like the media."

> —JIM RIGGLEMAN, *as the Cubs manager*

"The papers aren't going to win a game for me, and I don't need anybody to tell me I lost."

> —HARRY WALKER, *on never reading the newspapers*

"As long as I've got my cup on."

> —JIMY WILLIAMS, *on allowing the Red Sox press in the clubhouse early in the morning during spring training*

"I don't think that's so bad. I don't know why I didn't think of it."

> —TED WILLIAMS, *after Denny McClain poured water on the heads of two writers*

Mediocrity

"I'm going to play with harder nonchalance this year."

> —JACKIE BRANDT

"Baseball has been good to me since I quit trying to play it."

> —WHITEY HERZOG

"I'm a proven so-so player."

> —JEFF MANTO, *on playing for 10 different organizations in 14 years*

"I'm in the twilight of a mediocre career."

> —FRANK SULLIVAN

"It isn't the high price of stars that is expensive, it's the high price of mediocrity."

> —BILL VEECK

Meetings

"I've had managers who had 30-minute meetings but quit making sense after 30 seconds."

> —RICHIE HEBNER

"The only thing we led baseball in was team meetings."

> —RICHIE ZISK, *on a losing Mariners team*

Memorabilia

"In our day, you could have gotten a live catcher and his family for $975."

> —WAITE HOYT, *on a limited-edition sculpture of Johnny Bench selling for $975*

Mental Games

"You can't bat and think at the same time."

—YOGI BERRA

"I think too much on the mound sometimes and I get brain cramps."

—BRITT BURNS

"How could it be mental? I don't have a college education."

—STEVE FARR, *when asked if his shoulder soreness was mental*

"If you think long, you think wrong."

—JIM KAAT

"When the cerebral process enters into sports, you start screwing up."

—BILL LEE

"Trying to think with me is a mismatch. Hell, most of the time I don't know where the pitch is going."

—SAM MCDOWELL

"The only time we lose our concentration is when the umpire says, 'Play ball.'"

> —LOU PINIELLA, *when asked if his team was mentally prepared*

Metrodome

"You are a great pitcher with a 6.00 ERA in this dome."

> —JOAQUIN ANDUJAR, *on the Metrodome*

"It stinks. It's a shame a great guy like HHH has to be named after it."

> —BILLY MARTIN, *on the Hubert Horatio Humphrey Metrodome*

"I don't think there are good uses for nuclear weapons, but this place might be one."

> —DAN QUISENBERRY, *on the Metrodome*

Mets

"The Mets held a press conference and announced that all 1995 games would be played on the road."

> —DAVID LETTERMAN, *on how to increase attendance at Shea Stadium*

"I wouldn't want to come to the ballpark. If I were going to pay to see a baseball team, I'd pay to watch a good team."

> —BRET SABERHAGEN, *on a bad Mets team*

"I have a son and I make him watch the Mets. I want him to know life. It's a history lesson. He'll understand the Depression."

> —TOOTS SHOR, *famous restaurant owner, on the early years of the Mets*

"Our first Mets game was April 10, 1962, and it was our best game. It was rained out."

> —CASEY STENGEL, *on the early years of the Mets*

"We are a much-improved baseball club—now we lose in extra innings."

>—CASEY STENGEL, *during the early years of the Mets*

"The only thing worse than a Mets game is a Mets doubleheader."

>—CASEY STENGEL

"I'm not sure if I'd rather be managing or testing bulletproof vests."

>—JOE TORRE, *on the '81 Mets team, which he managed*

Mets Fans

"I'm not gonna give you any ammo."

>—JOHN ROCKER, *on attempting not to say anything bad about the Mets before the '99 playoffs*

"To hell with New York fans. They're a bunch of stupid asses."

>—JOHN ROCKER

Middle Relief

"A lot of long relievers are ashamed to tell their
parents what they do. The only nice thing about it is
you get to wear a uniform like everybody else."

—JIM BOUTON

"We call ourselves bottom feeders. The whole world
underappreciates middle relievers. . . . We pride
ourselves on being the plankton of the baseball
world."

—JEFF ZIMMERMAN, *middle reliever*

Minor Leagues

"I've been to every baseball park in America except
those in the American and National Leagues."

—RICK AMARAL, *career minor leaguer, on finally
making it to the majors at age 30*

"I took one giant step backwards."

—ROCKY BRIDGES, *on being demoted from
Triple-A ball to A ball*

"These teams in the Pacific Coast League were getting a little old. A couple of them wanted me to run for mayor."

> —DEWAYNE BUICE, *on being a career minor leaguer*

"I hate the minor leagues. I'd rather go out to lunch with my ex-wife's attorney than play in the minors."

> —DAVE COLLINS

"Back then you didn't sleep two to a room, you slept two to a bed. It was the first time I wore pajamas."

> —DAVE GARCIA, *on the minor leagues in the old days*

"Pawtucket is a much bigger city on the way up than it is on the way down."

> —GLENN HOFFMAN, *on the Red Sox sending him down to Pawtucket*

"What does it hurt to ask? All they can say is yes or no, and I already know the answer."

> —BILL PULSIPHER, *who asked the Mets if they would call him up from Triple-A, Norfolk*

"He has been doing well in Triple-A. He spent nine years in Triple-A; he should be doing well."

> —BOBBY VALENTINE, *on 29-year-old minor leaguer Mark Mimbs*

"No one will survive that many buses."

> —STAN WASIAK, *when asked if his record for the most wins by a minor-league manager will be eclipsed*

Money

"A nickel ain't worth a dime anymore."

> —YOGI BERRA

"If the guy was real poor, I'd give it back to him."

> —YOGI BERRA, *when asked what he would do if he found a million dollars*

"My father looked at the contract and then told the scout, 'Throw in another hundred and you can take the rest of the family.' "

>—JOE DUGAN, *on signing for $500 in the early 1920s*

"Any man who says he enjoys the game more than the money is fibbing."

>—WOODY FRYMAN

"The only way to make money as a manager is to win in one place, get fired, and get hired somewhere else."

>—WHITEY HERZOG

"Am I worth it? No. Is anybody?"

>—TODD JONES, *on signing a contract for $2.25 million in '98 and $2.95 million in '99*

"They say that a fool and his money are soon parted. I'd like to know how they got together in the first place."

>—BILL LEE

"Let's face it. It's not like they signed Christy Mathewson."

> —ROGER MCDOWELL, *on signing for $500,000 with Texas*

"I put all those people in the park who come to boo me."

> —AMOS OTIS, *explaining why he should make more money*

"Not really—they lean towards cash."

> —BILL VEECK, *when asked if free agents leaned toward big cities*

Moonwalk

"Two men land on the moon, and I got two guys who can't get to the ballpark."

> —LEO DUROCHER, *on two of his players showing up late for a game*

"When Neil Armstrong set foot on the moon, he found six baseballs that Jimmie Foxx hit off me in 1937."

—LEFTY GOMEZ

Movie Night

"She's already had so much experience grabbing herself, she should be great."

—JAY LENO, *on Madonna appearing in the movie A League of Their Own*

"I've played in more towns than *Gone with the Wind*."

—FRANK LUCCHESI, *on his many managerial jobs*

Music

"It was worse than trying out for the majors."

—JOHNNY BENCH, *on singing solo in a concert with the Cincinnati Symphony Orchestra*

"Where's the NRA when you need them?"

> —RON FAIRLY, *after the Expos' trumpeter played*
> *"The Happy Wanderer"*

"He wants to quit baseball and become a professional musician. The problem is he can't sing or play an instrument."

> —CARMEN FRANCO, *on her husband Julio*
> *wanting to retire from baseball*

"You could see the spitting, the groin pulling, and the scratching, or you could go to the ballpark."

> —DAVID LETTERMAN, *on a Madonna concert*
> *held across the street from a World Series*
> *game in Philadelphia*

MVP

"In 1962 I was named Minor League Player of the Year. It was my second season in the bigs."

> —BOB UECKER

N

Name Game

"I told [GM] Roland Hemond to go out and get me a big-name pitcher. He said, 'Dave Wehrmeister's got 11 letters. Is that a big enough name for you?'"

—EDDIE EICHORN, *White Sox owner*

"Joe is gone. He stinks. . . . Junior's a jerk, but at least he can play. In this game, you have to be a jerk."

—JUNIOR ORTIZ, *on changing his name to Joe for two weeks*

National Anthem

"Most of us have such bad voices, we respect the national anthem by not singing it."

—SPARKY ANDERSON

"You might be a redneck if you think the last words to 'The Star-Spangled Banner' are 'play ball'."

—JEFF FOXWORTHY

"Once the national anthem plays, I get chills. I even know the words to it now."

—PETE ROSE

Jerry Neudecker

"He's so incompetent that he couldn't be a crew chief on a sunken submarine."

—BILLY MARTIN, *on umpire Jerry Neudecker*

New York City

"Everything you hate about New York as a visitor you love as a home player."

—SCOTT BROSIUS

"I could not play in New York. The first time I ever came into a game there, I got into the bullpen cart and they told me to lock the door."

—MIKE FLANAGAN

"It's a tough job just being a coach in New York."

—TOM MCCRAW

"They told me to watch out for sharks. I saw a lot of bodies but no sharks."

—BOB SHIRLEY, *on a boat ride he took around New York after being acquired by the Yankees*

Phil Niekro

"I knew it was Phil Niekro's. I found his teeth in my glove compartment."

—MIKE FLANAGAN, *on a car the Blue Jays gave him*

Jim Northrup

"Jim Northrup in Detroit hated my guts. I didn't like him too much, either, but I played him."

—BILLY MARTIN

Oakland

"The only good thing about Oakland is that long bridge
that takes you directly into San Francisco."

—MUDCAT GRANT

Old-Timers' Games

"The older they get, the better they were when they
were younger."

—JIM BOUTON, *on old-timers*

"The real thrill in this game is to finish it."

—LOU BROCK, *on old-timers' games*

"Old-timers' games, weekends, and airplane landings are all alike. If you can walk away from them, they're successful."

—CASEY STENGEL

Olympic Stadium

"This place would make a good wine cellar."

—STEVE CARLTON, *on the cool 39-degree temperature in Montreal's Olympic Stadium*

"It always did look like a toilet bowl. Now it has a seat on it."

—WHITEY HERZOG, *on the roof built for Olympic Stadium*

"[Catching a ball on] that field is like trying to catch a Superball on asphalt."

—J. T. SNOW, *on the Olympic Stadium field*

Walter O'Malley

"The man has a cash register where a heart should be."

>—HOWARD COSELL, *on Walter O'Malley*

"He's the only guy I know who Dale Carnegie would hit in the mouth."

>—BILL VEECK, *on O'Malley*

Opening Day

"There are opening day pitchers and pitchers who start on opening day."

>—ROGER CRAIG

"If they had 75,000 fans in Cleveland in the opener, they must have passed out 300,000 free tickets."

>—GRAIG NETTLES, *on 75,000 fans showing up for opening day in Cleveland*

"When I saw Santa Claus in the first row, I knew this would be a strange day."

> —PAUL O'NEILL, *on a snowstorm that occurred on opening day at Yankee Stadium*

Options

"The workout is optional—whoever doesn't come gets optioned."

> —BOBBY VALENTINE

Orioles

"Their spirits are fine. I guess you guys [media] want a high school pom-pom team."

> —RAY MILLER, *on rumors that the Orioles' spirits were low during a losing streak*

"That team needs a Ping-Pong table more than any team I've ever seen."

> —ANDY VAN SLYKE, *on the lack of camaraderie on an Orioles team*

"We're so bad right now that for us back-to-back home runs means one today and one tomorrow."

—EARL WEAVER

Owners

"My position is that while the players don't deserve all that money, the owners don't deserve it even more."

—JIM BOUTON

"I'm going to write a book—*How to Make a Small Fortune in Baseball*. You start with a large fortune."

—RULY CARPENTER, *owner of the Philadelphia Phillies*

"I'm a typical owner. It doesn't matter what our record is just as long as I make money on the deal."

—KEVIN ELSTER, *on buying interest in an Independent League team*

"If some of the owners had a brain, they'd be idiots."

—CHARLIE FINLEY, *on baseball owners*

"I don't want to be sitting next to some author or Bing Crosby's son telling me how to manage."

> —JIM LEYLAND, *on enjoying working with nonintrusive Marlins owner Wayne Huizenga*

"Baseball must be a great game because the owners haven't been able to kill it."

> —BILL VEECK

"The dumbest NFL owner is equal to the smartest baseball owner."

> —EDWARD BENNETT WILLIAMS

P

Padres

"I get tired of having my ballplayers bellyache all the time. They should sit in the press box sometime and watch themselves play."

—BUZZIE BAVASI, *on Padres players*

"I would never want to be a Padre. I mean, how do you get into the Hall of Fame as a Padre?"

—REGGIE JACKSON, *on free agents signing with teams with no tradition*

"There is some good news and bad news. First the good news: you loyal fans outdid Los Angeles [in attendance]. Now the bad news: I have never seen such stupid ballplaying in my life."

>—RAY KROC, *owner of the Padres, on the '74 home opener*

"The club is a lot of fun, like my wife, but there is no profit in either one."

>—RAY KROC, *on the Padres*

"With the Padres, you'd get off to a 3–1 start, and that would be the baseball highlight of the season."

>—STEVE MURA

Padres Fans

"They don't know baseball here. In other places, they don't boo me. They enjoy my game."

>—BENITO SANTIAGO, *on Padres fans*

Dave Parker

"That's pretty good considering Dave's previous idol was himself."

> —WILLIE STARGELL, *on Dave Parker saying Stargell was his idol*

Phillies

"I'll play first, third, left . . . I'll play anywhere except Philadelphia."

> —DICK ALLEN

"That's too bad—they are the only team I can beat."

> —DAVID COLES, *on being traded to the Phillies in the mid-'50s*

"You'd invite this team over for dinner, but you'd cover your furniture with plastic before we arrive."

> —JOHN KRUK, *on the '93 Phillies team*

"Every Mormon has a missionary obligation, and Murph's is fulfilling his with this lowlife team."

>—JOHN KRUK, *on Dale Murphy*

"We're 24 morons and a Mormon."

>—JOHN KRUK, *on the Phillies with Dale Murphy*

"I'm 49 years old, and I'd like to live to be 50."

>—EDDIE SAWYER, *on why he quit as the manager of the Phillies*

Phillies Fans

"Phillie fans would boo a wake."

>—JOE DUGAN

"Some of the people would boo the crack in the Liberty Bell."

>—PETE ROSE, *on Phillies fans*

"Philadelphia is the only city in the world where you can experience the thrill of victory and the agony of reading about it the next day."

> —MIKE SCHMIDT

"You know what they do when the game's rained out? They go to the airport and boo landings."

> —BOB UECKER, *on Phillies fans*

Pirates

"Baseball is supposed to be a noncontact sport, but our hitters seem to be taking that literally."

> —LARRY DOUGHTY, *Pirates GM*

"I didn't think it was Death Valley—I thought it was Dead Valley."

> —ANDY VAN SLYKE, *on the morale of the team when he first joined the Pirates*

"You can't ask Mr. Ed to keep up with Secretariat."

> —ANDY VAN SLYKE, *on the Pirates trying to catch up to the rest of the division*

Pirates Fans

"There's only about 5,000 of them. How can you miss them?"

> —BARRY BONDS, *when asked if he heard boos every time he came up to bat*

"They're all Rotisserie League geeks who don't have the slightest idea how to play the game except on a computer."

> —JASON KENDALL, *angry at fans for booing teammate Al Martin*

Pitchers

"They're the only players in the game allowed to cheat. They throw illegal pitches and they sneak foreign substances on the ball."

> —RICHIE ASHBURN

"One day you can throw tomatoes through brick walls. The next day you can't dent a piece of glass with a rock."

—DEAN CHANCE

"I was never nervous when I had the ball, but when I let it go, I was scared to death."

—LEFTY GOMEZ

"We need three kinds of pitching—left-handed, right-handed, and relief."

—WHITEY HERZOG, *on the Cardinals' desperate need for some solid pitching*

"Pitchers aren't athletes."

—CHUCK HILLER

"He's left-handed and he's breathing."

—TOM KELLY, *on what he liked about a particular pitching prospect*

"I made some dumb pitches when I had to."

—DAVE LAPOINT, *explaining why he lost a game*

"The only thing wrong with our pitchers is that they all have to pitch on the same night."

—DON OSBORN, *Pirates pitching coach*

"Our pitching staff is a conspiracy of *if*s."

—BRANCH RICKEY

"I can hit any pitcher alive—if he stands still."

—RICHIE SCHEINBLUM

Pitchers Hitting

"I know his weakness. He can't hit."

—WHITEY FORD, *when asked if there was something Sandy Koufax couldn't do*

"One good night does not a hitter make."

—TOM GLAVINE, *on John Smoltz getting two good hits in a game*

"Even a blind dog finds a bone every once in a while."

—BRUCE HURST, *on a rare hit*

"I'll miss hitting. I like making a fool out of myself with a bat."

> —BRUCE KISON, *on being traded to the American League*

"I used to be so bad, my bat would close its eyes when I came up."

> —JERRY KOOSMAN

"Joaquin Andujar and a curveball at the plate are complete strangers."

> —TOMMY LASORDA

"Most great power hitters don't hit for high averages."

> —TERRY MULHOLLAND, *on his second career home run lifting his batting average to around .100*

"To show I have power to all fields."

> —TERRY MULHOLLAND, *explaining why he wanted to hit his third home run to right field. One of his previous homers went to left and the other to center.*

"They're so bad, I won't even let them take batting practice anymore."

—JOHNNY OATES, *on some of the Rangers pitchers who were attempting to get ready for interleague play by taking batting practice*

"I have no clue what any of this means. For all I know, we don't even have signs."

—TROY PERCIVAL, *Angels pitcher, on batting during interleague play*

Pitching Changes

"Well, I'm tired of you."

—CASEY STENGEL, *when a pitcher told him that he didn't want to leave the game because he wasn't tired*

Planes, Trains, and Automobiles

"I don't know why the players make such a fuss about sitting in the first-class section of the plane. Does that mean they'll get there faster?"

—SPARKY ANDERSON

Player of the Month

"I have mixed emotions. I think I may be in line for Player of the Month in the Florida State League."

—TOMMY JOHN, *on being called up to the Yankees in mid-August after a rehab stint in the Florida State League*

Player of the Week

"That just shows you how this league has gone to hell."

—CHUCK FINLEY, *on being named the Player of the Week*

"I guess there have been some bad players in the American League this week."

> —WALT TERRELL, *on being named the Player of the Week*

Playoffs

"The Los Angeles Rams."

> —LEO DUROCHER, *when asked whom he liked in the playoffs, after the Mets beat the Cubs to win the division*

Please Release Me

"They can ship me to Alaska if they want. They can send me home tomorrow if they like. I'll watch the boys play from my house."

> —BOBBY BONILLA, *on how he would feel if he was released by the Mets*

"Whenever I decided to release a guy, I always had his room searched for a gun. You couldn't take any chances with some of these birds."

> —CASEY STENGEL

"Son, we'd like to keep you around this season, but we're going to try to win a pennant."

> —CASEY STENGEL, *cutting prospect Aubrey Gatewood from the team*

Politics

"I can tell my grandchildren that I pitched to John Kennedy at Harvard."

> —LEW KRAUSE, *on the Red Sox working out at Harvard and Krause pitching to Red Sox utility player John Kennedy*

"What do I need Humphrey for? He can't hit."

> —EDDIE STANKY, *explaining why he didn't want Vice President Humphrey to visit the White Sox clubhouse during a game*

Postseason

"Was it my biggest postseason moment? It was my only postseason moment."

> —CASEY CANDAELE, *on walking as an Indian during the '96 playoffs*

Potty Talk

"Raise the urinals."

> —DARREL CHANEY, *when asked how to keep the Braves on their toes*

Practice

"I got blisters for swinging eight billion times in practice, then I go 0-for-5 in the game."

> —STEVE LYONS

"I tried real hard not to get any muscles so I wouldn't hurt them."

> —DAN QUISENBERRY, *when asked about practicing in the off-season*

Predictions

"The only guys not picking us last are our writers, because they know they have to deal with us. They're picking us fifth."

> —TOM PAGNOZZI, *on the Cardinals*

Pregnant Pause

"He only missed by one."

> —VIN SCULLY, *after Rennie Stennett, whose wife had not yet given birth, prematurely gave out cigars saying "It's a boy" and the baby turned out to be a girl*

Problems

"The problem with telling people you have problems is 80 percent of the people don't give a damn and the other 20 percent are glad you have them."

—TOMMY LASORDA

Prospects

"The kid doesn't chew tobacco, smoke, drink, curse, or chase broads. I don't see how he can possibly make it."

—RICHIE ASHBURN, *on an up-and-coming prospect*

Public Appearance

"I don't walk the streets."

—BRUCE KISON, *when asked how often he was recognized on the street*

Q

Quiet Man

"Johnny Sain doesn't say much, but that doesn't matter much, because when you're out there on the mound, you got nobody to talk to."

—CASEY STENGEL, *on Sain*

R

Rainout

"We lost 13 straight one year. I decided if we got rained out, we'd throw a victory party."

—LEFTY GOMEZ, *on a minor-league team he managed*

Rangers

"We're not as bad as people thought, although that's not saying much."

—BUDDY BELL, *on the Rangers*

"Same old Texas Rangers. We score a lot of runs and see if the pitching survives."

> —DOUG MELVIN, *Rangers GM, after the Rangers lost a big lead*

"We set the tables, but no one ate."

> —JOHNNY OATES, *after the Rangers left 14 runners on base in a game*

"They never considered the Rangers a major-league team anyway."

> —KENNY ROGERS, *on his family being pleased he was signed by the Yankees and leaving the Rangers*

Records

"I've never had a club record except for car wrecks."

> —DARREN DAULTON, *on breaking the Phillies' record for the most RBIs by a catcher*

"I don't like that record. You can have it."

> —ANDRES GALLARAGA, *on setting a Braves record by being hit by a pitch 21 times during a season*

Red Sox

"Our pain isn't as bad as you might think. Dead bodies don't suffer."

> —BILL LEE, *on the '78 Red Sox collapse*

"At my stupidest, I was never as stupid as the Boston Red Sox."

> —TED TURNER, *on paying outrageous salaries for players in the early '80s*

Red Sox Fans

"The people have no manners. They have no respect for anything. They raise their kids to get on people."

> —BILL BUCKNER, *on Red Sox fans*

Reds

"If the Cincinnati Reds were really the first major-league baseball team, who did they play?"

—GEORGE CARLIN

"We got a lot of guys not doing what their bubble-gum card says they can do."

—RAY KNIGHT

"The Cincinnati Reds are like a drill team—they should be managed by Jack Webb."

—BILL LEE, *on the Big Red Machine*

"I went to church the other day to pray for our pitchers. But there weren't enough candles."

—JACK MCKEON, *on the '98 Reds*

"I don't know if we've reached the highest level of embarrass-tivity, but we've sure been embarrassed."

—JOSE RIJO, *on a fight breaking out on the team between him and Chris Sabo*

Relief in Sight

"It's kind of like being in a *Rocky* movie—you get to start over every year."

—ROB DIBBLE, *on being a relief pitcher*

"Whoever answers the bullpen phone."

—CHUCK ESTRADA, *Rangers pitching coach, on how he chooses who will be the relief pitcher*

"We're parasites. We live off the people who spend two hours on the field."

—DAN QUISENBERRY, *on relief pitchers*

"The bullpen is a nice place to visit, but I wouldn't want to live there."

—BILL SINGER, *on being a starting pitcher*

"I have an idea what to do about the bullpen—napalm."

—STAN WILLIAMS, *pitching coach for the Mariners, on suggestions for improving a bad relief corps*

Religion

"If it was that easy, Billy Graham would hit .400."

> —CHRIS SABO, *on Marge Schott saying the Reds should pray to end their losing streak*

"I'd rather walk with the bases loaded."

> —EARL WEAVER, *after player Pat Kelly asked Weaver to walk with the Lord*

Resignation

"It was like water torture. It just kept dripping and dripping."

> —MARCEL LACHEMANN, *after resigning as the Angels manager after posting a 52–59 record*

Retirement

"They were starting to hit the dry side of the ball."

> —LEW BURDETTE, *a pitcher notorious for using a spitball, on why he decided to retire*

"I don't want to be in your future. It's frustrating enough being in your present."

> —ROGER ERICKSON, *Yankees pitcher,*
> *addressing Yankees management when*
> *deciding to retire instead of being demoted to*
> *the minors*

"I'd become a professional go-getter. My wife would go to work, and I'd go get her."

> —TIM FLANNERY, *on what he planned to do*
> *when he retired*

"Probably rest for about ten years and then figure out something to do."

> —JOHN KRUK, *on his retirement plans*

"I got tired of ducking line drives and backing up home plate."

> —BOB MILLER, *explaining why he decided to*
> *retire*

"In one day, I went from a negative presence to a man with a great past."

> —JIM PALMER, *on his retirement from baseball*

"My arm has felt so bad since I retired that I can't even throw a tantrum."

> —STEVE STONE

Branch Rickey

"Rickey has both money and players. He just didn't like to see the two of them meet."

> —CHUCK CONNORS, *on Branch Rickey*

"He'd go into the vault to get you a nickel change."

> —ENOS SLAUGHTER, *on Rickey*

"I got a million dollars' worth of advice and a very small raise."

> —EDDIE STANKY, *on negotiating with Branch Rickey*

Rivalries

"Do the Yankees like the Red Sox?"

> —GARY KASPAROV, *champion chess player, when asked if he liked his chief rival, Anatoly Karpov*

Road Trips

"I lost the bus and two outfielders, but I won a shortstop and a bat."

> —ROCKY BRIDGES, *describing a road trip in the minor leagues when the team got lost on the way to San Jose*

"There wasn't much of a delay. We only had to change a spark plug and 30 pairs of shorts."

> —DON DRYSDALE, *on the Dodgers' private jet having to make an emergency landing*

"On the road, if you go downstairs for coffee in your underwear, they throw you out of the kitchen."

> —ANDY VAN SLYKE, *on the difference between playing on the road and at home*

Rockies

"It's not going to take someone launching the shuttle at Cape Canaveral to realize we have a deficiency against left-handed pitchers."

> —CLINT HURDLE, *Rockies hitting coach, on his team's inability to beat lefties*

Rock 'n' Roll

"Rock-and-roll musicians don't step on stage and get booed."

> —JACK MCDOWELL, *on the difference between playing in a rock band and baseball*

Mel Rojas

"Mr. Excuse is probably in there making up another excuse."

> —KEVIN MALONE, *Expos GM, on another blown save by Mel Rojas*

Roommates

"How would you like to be married to Miss Connecticut and wake up every morning and look at Pod?"

> —BILLY GARDNER, *Twins manager, on rooming with pitching coach Johnny Podres while being married to a former Miss Connecticut*

Rotisserie League

"The proper way to end a conversation with a Roto guy is by saying, 'Get a life.'"

> —TONY KORNHEISER, *on Rotisserie League players*

Rules

"We live by the golden rule. Those who have the gold make the rules."

—BUZZIE BAVASI

"I try not to break the rules but merely test their elasticity."

—BILL VEECK

"If we're not going to play by the rules, there's no sense having a rule book."

—EARL WEAVER, *after tearing up a rule book in front of an umpire*

Bill Russell

"I told Bill to bear down, because those games count on my record."

—TOMMY LASORDA, *who was out after heart surgery, on what he said to Bill Russell, the acting manager in his absence*

Babe Ruth

"Santa Claus drinking his whiskey straight and groaning from a bellyache."

—JIMMY CANNON, *on Babe Ruth*

"If you cut that big slob in half, most of the concessions at Yankee Stadium would be pouring out."

—WAITE HOYT

"I'll have to go with the immoral Babe Ruth."

—JOHNNY LOGAN, *when asked who was the greatest player of all time*

"If it wasn't for baseball, I'd be in either the penitentiary or the cemetery."

—BABE RUTH

Dick Ruthven

"The kid's got good stuff, but I don't know why he doesn't throw it at anybody but us."

> —RED SCHOENDIENST, *on Dick Ruthven having a great record against the Cardinals but a dismal record against everyone else*

S

Safeco Field

"No lead is Safe-co Field."

> —ANONYMOUS, *proposing a nickname for Safeco Field*

"If you want to send someone to the minors around here, he can hide for a week."

> —LOU PINIELLA, *on the size of the clubhouses at Safeco Field*

San Francisco

"The coldest winter I ever spent was a summer in San Francisco."

> —CHARLIE DRESSEN

Deion Sanders

"Down in Atlanta, they have a guy they call Prime Time. In San Diego, they call me No Time."

—DANN BILARDELLO, *comparing himself to Deion Sanders*

"He's basically a glorified flag-football player who can run."

—CURT SCHILLING, *on Sanders's baseball talents*

Ron Santo

"Five runs ahead and he'd knock in all the runs I could ask for. One run behind and he was going to kill me."

—LEO DUROCHER

Steve Sax

"First I pray to God that nobody hits the ball to me.
Then I pray to God nobody hits the ball to Steve Sax."

—PEDRO GUERRERO, *on Sax's defensive
shortcomings*

Marge Schott

"The only thing I don't like is when the dog takes a
crap at shortstop, because I might have to dive into
that shi—."

—BARRY LARKIN, *on Marge Schott and her dog,
Schotzie*

"Mother Nature is my least favorite female. I won't say
who it used to be."

—MARK PORTUGAL, *on several rainouts in a row
and, prior to that, having a falling-out with
Marge Schott*

Scouts

"When a scout tells you a player can't miss, don't listen."

—PAUL RICHARDS

"All they do is watch games."

—MARGE SCHOTT, *complaining about the scouts in the Reds organization*

Seats

"They were so high, I could high-five with the guys in the blimp."

—TOMMY LASORDA, *on bad seats he had for a game*

"I have discovered, in 20 years of my being around a ballpark, that the knowledge of the game is usually in inverse proportion to the price of the seat."

—BILL VEECK

Seattle

"Seattle is not a baseball city; it is a coffee stand with computer geeks chatting over scones."

> —RICK TELANDER

Second Place

"We had a case of Ripple on ice."

> —JOHN FELSKE, *after the Phillies made it to second place in their division by winning the last game of the season*

Senators

"The fans like to see home runs, and we have assembled a pitching staff for their enjoyment."

> —CLARK GRIFFITH, *owner of the Washington Senators*

"The Senators were never very good, but not much has changed in Washington. The senators they have there still aren't very good."

—RICHARD NIXON, *after the Washington Senators moved out*

Seventh-Inning Stretch

"In the seventh inning, the fans get up and sing, 'Take Me Out to the Ball Game,' and you're already there. It's really a stupid thing to sing."

—LARRY ANDERSEN

Shaved Heads

"If this keeps up, you might see me without any body hair."

—JOEY HAMILTON, *on bombing in the first two starts and shaving his head to change his luck—only to be bombed again*

"I'd consider it myself, but my ears are too big. I'd look like a cab whose doors are open."

> —JIM LEYLAND, *on Dante Bichette shaving his head*

Shutouts

"What we could use is a couple of shutouts, but I don't even know if that would be good enough to win."

> —WHITEY HERZOG, *on the anemic Cardinals offense*

"That is usually what I've done—done good for one week a year."

> —WALT TERRELL, *on posting two shutouts in a week*

Sign Man

"They want to test my patience. I'm going to test their checkbook."

> —RENE LACHEMANN, *Marlins manager, on fining Kurt Abbott for missing a bunt sign*

"If they were any simpler, I'd be using flash cards."

>—DICK WILLIAMS, *on the signs he creates for players*

Singles

"If I had as many singles as Pete Rose, I'd have worn a dress."

>—MICKEY MANTLE

"If I'd just tried for them dinky singles, I could've batted around .600."

>—BABE RUTH

Sinkerballs

"The batter still hits a grounder. But in this case the first bounce is 360 feet away."

>—DAN QUISENBERRY, *on what happens when his sinker is not working*

"Natural grass is a wonderful thing for little bugs—and sinkerball pitchers."

> —DAN QUISENBERRY

Size-Wise

"Fred Patek was so small that when he was born his father passed out cigar butts."

> —JOEY ADAMS, *on the short former Royals shortstop*

"We have baked potatoes in North Carolina that are bigger than him."

> —GREG BOOKER, *on tiny Bip Roberts*

"The Little Twerp."

> —TOM GLAVINE, *on what his nickname should be when facing the Big Unit, Randy Johnson*

Sliders

"I can't find my slider. I have to hire someone to find it for me. I've got to hire a detective guy."

> —JOSE RIJO, *on reversing his fortunes during a tough year*

"I can't throw one, so I bought one."

> —CURT SCHILLING, *on buying a dog and naming it Slider*

Slow Stuff

"Nobody knows how fast I am. The ball doesn't get to the mitt that often."

> —LEFTY GOMEZ

"I think he throws harder than me."

> —CHARLIE HOUGH, *after Joe DiMaggio threw out a ball at the Marlins' first game as a team*

"The harder you throw, the less time you have to duck."

> —DOUG JONES, *on the advantages of throwing slow*

"I knew I was in trouble when they started clocking my fastball with a sundial."

> —JOE MAGRANE

"I don't throw hard enough to get a sore arm."

> —DALE MOHORIC, *on the concern about his developing a sore arm because he appeared in 15 of the first 17 games of a season*

"If overconfidence can cause the Roman Empire to fall, I ought to be able to get a ground ball."

> —DAN QUISENBERRY, *on batters' overconfidence because of the slow speed of Quisenberry's delivery*

"You could almost walk alongside them."

> —LON SIMMONS, *A's announcer, on the slow pitches of Tommy John*

"In the '70s I threw in the 90s. In the '90s, I throw in the 70s."

> —FRANK TANANA

"You can time his stuff with a squirt gun."

> —DAVE WINFIELD, *on the pitching of DeWayne Buice*

Slumps

"I wish I had an answer to that, because I'm tired of answering that question."

> —YOGI BERRA, *on a Yankees slump*

"I'm the only man in the history of the game who began his career in a slump and stayed in it."

> —ROCKY BRIDGES

"Nobody's nice to me anymore. . . . All they throw me are curves, and they know I can't hit them."

> —ENOS CABELL, *on a slump*

"In baseball there are only two things I'm an expert on—trades and slumps."

> —JOE GARAGIOLA

"A string of alibis."

> —MILLER HUGGINS, *on what players need during a slump*

"You're like a mosquito in a nudist camp. You don't know where to start."

> —REGGIE JACKSON, *on the many ideas he has for breaking out of a slump*

"On a team that is 40 games under .500, I don't feel like I'm being persecuted."

> —MATT KEOUGH, *when asked if he felt he was being persecuted because of his 0–11 record*

"When it rains, it pours, and we're in the midst of a monsoon."

> —RAY KNIGHT, *on a Reds losing streak*

"When you're in a slump, it's almost as if you look out at the field and it's one big glove."

> —VANCE LAW

"We gotta trade him while he's still hot."

> —CASEY STENGEL, *on Don Zimmmer getting two hits in a row after an 0-for-34 slump*

"I had slumps that lasted into winter."

> —BOB UECKER

"The thing is, a lot of the people who make these suggestions would have a hard time filling out the application forms to work at 7-Eleven."

> —ANDY VAN SLYKE, *on advice he received during a slump*

"I have an Alka-Seltzer bat. You know, plop, plop, fizz, fizz. When the pitcher sees me walking up there, they say, 'Oh, what a relief it is.'"

> —ANDY VAN SLYKE, *during a slump*

Small Towns

"The population is about 250. That counts the pregnant people twice."

—DAVID WEATHERS, *on his hometown of Five Points, Tennessee*

Soap Dish

"Your body is just like a bar of soap. It gradually wears down after repeated use."

—DICK ALLEN

Softball

"When we played softball, I'd steal second base, feel guilty, and go back."

—WOODY ALLEN

"He was an idiot doing something else. I'm not calling him an idiot, but it was an idiot thing he was doing."

> —BOBBY VALENTINE, *on Jason Isringhausen playing softball while recovering from an injury*

Speed Demon

"There was larceny in his heart, but his feet were honest."

> —BUGS BAER, *on the slow-footed Ping Bodie*

"There was nothing to lose."

> —RON FAIRLY, *at age 39, when asked if he had lost any speed*

"Jesse Owens never won a baseball game in his life."

> —JIM KAAT, *on why he doesn't practice wind sprints*

"I only have one speed, and it has never changed—that speed is very slow."

> —BROOKS ROBINSON

"His only limitation is his ability to move around."

> —JOE TORRE, *on Pedro Guerrero*

"I don't know if I could beat him running backwards, but it would be close."

> —LARRY WALKER, *on the slow-footed Darrin Fletcher*

"Rich Dauer is so slow that we time him from home to first with a calendar."

> —EARL WEAVER

Spelunking

"The first time I heard about spelunking, I thought it had something to do with pornography."

> —TREVOR HOFFMAN, *on his contract, which specifies that he cannot go spelunking (cave exploring)*

Spitters

"When I have fingers run through my hair, I usually get kissed."

> —DON DRYSDALE, *on umpire Augie Donatelli rubbing his fingers through Drysdale's hair looking for an illegal substance*

"It was so cold that ice was forming on my spitter."

> —DICK FARRELL, *on a 30-degree game*

"I never threw the spitter—well, maybe once or twice when I really needed to get a guy out real bad."

> —WHITEY FORD

"Not intentionally, but I sweat easily."

> —LEFTY GOMEZ, *when asked if he threw a spitter*

"The league will be a little drier now."

> —GAYLORD PERRY, *on his retirement*

"When I was a little boy, my mother warned me never to stick my dirty fingers in my mouth."

—PHIL REGAN, *denying that he threw spitters*

"Clean living and the spitball."

—PREACHER ROE, *explaining his longevity in baseball*

Sportswriters

"There are 300,000 sportswriters, and they're all against me. Every one of them."

—JOAQUIN ANDUJAR

"The Lord taught me to love everybody, but the last ones I learned to love were the sportswriters."

—ALVIN DARK

"The hell with sportswriters. You can buy any of them with a steak."

—GEORGE WEISS

Spring Training

"There are plenty of Hank Aarons in spring training."

—BOBBY COX, *on all the great prospects in spring training*

"The way you make coaches think you're in shape in the spring is to get a tan."

—WHITEY FORD

"Spring training should last one day. We'd have the team golf outing and head north."

—JOHN KRUK

"I guess they'll be getting a lot of take signs."

—EDGAR MARTINEZ, *on the Mariners showing up for a split-squad game without bats*

"Last year at this time, we might have had Tom and Jerry, a couple of mice, out there. This year, look at all the people."

—GREGG OLSEN, *on the Braves' spring training facility the year after they went from last place to first*

"That's great—we'll take 29 players and let the muggers make our final cuts."

> —BOBBY VALENTINE, *on the Mets playing in New Orleans during the preseason*

"To tell you the truth, I couldn't stand to see us on the field anymore."

> —DICK WILLIAMS, *on arbitrarily deciding to end an Angels spring training game after eight innings*

Stats

"Statistics are about as interesting as first-base coaches."

> —JIM BOUTON

"They have statistics for everything, even which nostril is running."

> —JOHN MCNAMARA

George Steinbrenner

"You know, throughout the World Series it was really a team victory, and the team played so well George Steinbrenner is really not sure who he's going to fire."

> —DAVID LETTERMAN, *after the Yankees won the '96 World Series*

"Nothing is more limited than being a limited partner of George's."

> —JIM MCMULLEN, *on being a limited owner of the Yankees*

"I don't know, but if he does, I want to be the owner."

> —GENE MICHAEL, *when asked if George would ever become a major-league manager*

"He has nothin' to do with nothin'."

> —DAVE WINFIELD, *on Steinbrenner*

Stolen Base

"I couldn't resist. I had such a great jump on the pitcher."

> —LOU NOVIKOFF, *on trying to steal third with the bases loaded*

"Can't make a racehorse out of a mule."

> —HARRY SPILMAN, *on going seven years without a stolen base*

"I could hear him coming. I was dumbfounded. I didn't know how to act."

> —TIM TSCHIDA, *second-base umpire, on watching Cecil Fielder steal his first base in 906 games*

Streaks

"I'm superstitious. Every night after I got a hit I ate Tex-Mex food and drank tequila. I had to stop hitting or die."

> —TIM FLANNERY, *on the end of his hitting streak*

"It took me 12 years to become an overnight sensation."

> —TOBY HARRAH, *during a hitting streak*

"This isn't a salary drive—it's a survival drive."

> —JAMIE QUIRK, *on a hitting streak*

Stretch Run

"You don't want guys asking questions down the stretch. You want them having answers."

> —BOBBY VALENTINE, *on having experienced players on the team at the end of season*

Strike

"The only thing that keeps you going is that at least every morning you wake up and you're still in first place by half a game."

> —JIM BOWDEN, *Reds GM, during the '94 strike*

"The owners are about to shut down baseball, which is more prosperous than it's ever been, and the players are the ones who have to get their urine tested."

—RON DARLING, *on the 1994 baseball strike*

"I don't anticipate any of them going out and getting jobs. A few might have to fire their gardeners and chauffeurs."

—DALLAS GREEN, *on the effect the 1994 strike would have on the players*

"They don't hit fast pitches, they don't have a 90-foot range, they miss aluminum bats, and they can't drive past a Pizza Hut without stopping."

—RENE LACHEMANN, *describing replacement players on the Marlins*

"I was about to wave off the guy who came up to squeegee my windshield, but then I realized it was Don Mattingly."

—DAVID LETTERMAN, *on the impact of the '94 strike*

"If there is a hell, it's a small room in which one is trapped for eternity with both of these men."

> —ROBERT REICH, *former Clinton labor secretary, on trying to negotiate a settlement to end a baseball strike and having to deal with Donald Fehr and Bud Selig*

"I don't walk no picket lines. I've got more important things to do than stand outside a stadium and take abuse from fans."

> —BRET SABERHAGEN, *on his decision to not picket during the '94 strike*

"It's like if you went to New York for an opera expecting Pavarotti, and the curtain opens and Rosanne is sitting there."

> —DAVID SEGUI, *on replacement players*

Strikeout

"Keep it. I don't want it."

> —RAY CHAPMAN, *said after Walter Johnson threw two quick strikes against him and he started walking away from the batter's box*

"It's lighter to carry back to the dugout after I strike out."

> —ERNIE FAZIO, *on the advantage of going to a lighter bat*

"He passed me on the all-time strikeout list a couple of years ago and nobody asked me about that."

> —MICKEY MANTLE, *when asked how he felt after Reggie Jackson passed him on the all-time home-run list*

"A guy who strikes out as much as I do had better lead in something."

> —MIKE SCHMIDT, *on leading the league in homers*

"I put tiptoes in the back of the batter's box and couldn't wait until my three pitches were over."

> —BOB UECKER, *on facing Don Drysdale*

Superstitions

"For five years in the minor leagues, I wore the same underwear and still hit .250—so no, I don't believe in that stuff."

—DUSTY BAKER, *on superstitions*

"Superstitious? These guys aren't superstitious. They're just too cheap to send out their laundry."

—TOM TRESH

Swing Away

"The only time I saw Alfredo walk was to the bus."

—DAVE COLLINS, *on Alfredo Griffin never walking*

Swingers

"Anybody can hit with a good swing. Try to hit with my swing."

—TIM FOLI, *on his .249 lifetime batting average*

T

Talk Is Cheap

"That's why I don't talk. Because I talk too much."

—JOAQUIN ANDUJAR

Tapes

"It's like when you go into the record store and there's that rack of tapes selling for $2.99. You look through it and look through it, trying to find a good one. Well, somehow I got put on that rack."

—DON CARMEN, *on signing for the major-league base salary of $500,000*

Tax Fraud

"The feds can kiss my ass."

—DARRYL STRAWBERRY, *on his tax-fraud case*

Teamwork

"Winning isn't as important as doing well individually. You can't take teamwork up to the front office to negotiate."

—KEN LANDREAUX

"You may have the greatest bunch of individual stars in the world, but if they don't play together, the club won't be worth a dime."

—BABE RUTH

Television

"Doing TV backup games is like hosting a telethon for hiccups."

—RON LUCIANO

Temper, Temper

"I just don't have that first-step explosion anymore."

> —LOU PINIELLA, *on tripping on a dugout step when going to argue a call with an umpire*

"I'm not stupid. I didn't punch it with my pitching hand."

> —RON VILLONE, *left-handed Reds pitcher, who hit a wall with his right hand during a temper tantrum*

Third Base

"They want me to play third like Brooks Robinson, but I think I play it more like Mel Brooks."

> —TIM FLANNERY

Three Rivers Stadium

"My father's cemetery has more life in it than this ballpark."

—RICHIE HEBNER, *whose dad owned a cemetery, on Three Rivers Stadium*

Marv Throneberry

"Having Marv Throneberry play for your team is like having Willie Sutton play for your bank."

—JIMMY BRESLIN, *on "Marvelous" Marv Throneberry*

Tiger Stadium

"They don't have a father-son game here because the kids would get lost."

—GRAIG NETTLES, *on the length of the grass on the field at Tiger Stadium*

Tigers

"It could be worse. He could be in Detroit."

> —DAVID CONE, *on Cecil Fielder complaining about his utility role with the Yankees*

Tough Outs

"Well, I got my man."

> —DON LIDDLE, *the pitcher who threw the ball during the game in which Willie Mays made the famous catch against Vic Wertz*

Trade Winds

"Yeah, that's true. I can see why he got out of the business."

> —HAROLD BAINES, *on George W. Bush saying the stupidest thing he ever did was trade Sammy Sosa for Harold Baines*

"We played him, and then we couldn't trade him."

> —BUZZIE BAVASI, *on Don Zimmer's ultimatum of
> "play me or trade me"*

**"I've had more numbers on my back then a bingo
board."**

> —ROCKY BRIDGES, *on his many teams*

"We picked up breakfast, and they picked up dinner."

> —NED COLLETTI, *Giants assistant GM, on Rich
> DeLucia being traded by the Giants to the
> Angels, who were staying at the same hotel*

**"I never pay attention to what ballplayers say. It's just
their way of getting newspaper ink."**

> —ALVIN DARK, *on a player who requested to be
> traded*

**"The talent we would have to potentially give up would
leave us with a team that Roger Clemens would not
want to play for."**

> —GERRY HUNSICKER, *Astros GM, on why the
> Astros decided not to trade for Roger Clemens*

"It wasn't that bad a deal. Ellingsen turned out to be the best liquor salesman in California."

> —TOMMY LASORDA, *on the Dodgers trading Bruce Ellingsen for Pedro Guerrero*

"I have found that every five years a man has to change his Sox."

> —STEVE LYONS, *on being traded to the Red Sox in 1991, after five years with the White Sox*

"I'm never one to bear a grudge. If I did, I'd hate half the teams in the American League."

> —PAUL MIRABELLA, *when asked if he resented being cut by the Mariners*

"Work hard, eat right, sleep right. And thank God there are 30 teams."

> —MIKE MORGAN, *on his secret to lasting in the major leagues for years and playing on many teams*

"No. Every team I throw against is my ex-team."

> —MIKE MORGAN, *when asked if he would be inspired to beat the Twins, his former team*

"I'd have a nice sports bar full of jerseys with 'Murphy' on the back."

> —ROB MURPHY, *on playing for eight different teams*

"I'm not sure which is more insulting, being offered in a trade or having it turned down."

> —CLAUDE OSTEEN

"We tried to get the Phillie Phanatic for Luis Polonia, but the Phillies wouldn't do it."

> —RAFAEL PALMIERO, *as an Oriole*

"No one knows this, but one of us has just been traded to Kansas City."

> —CASEY STENGEL, *on how he let Bob Cerv know he had been traded*

"Maybe they'll trade me for a bag of balls."

> —BOB TEWKSBURY, *on rumors of him being traded near the end of his career while he was on the disabled list*

"I think when it comes to trades, the American League is 98 percent air and about 2 percent balloon."

> —SYD THRIFT

Travelin' Man

"Why buy good luggage? You only use it when you travel."

> —YOGI BERRA

Triple Plays

"Joe Morgan [the manager] told me we had to stay out of double plays, and we did."

> —DENNIS LAMP, *on the Red Sox hitting into two triple plays in a game*

"It's like landing on the moon."

> —JODY REED, *on hitting the ball that led to the second triple play in that same game*

"I wouldn't mind seeing someone erase my record of hitting into four triple plays."

—BROOKS ROBINSON, *on all of his records*

Triples

"It replaced the Kentucky Derby as the most exciting two minutes in sports."

—DAVE BAKER, *Atlanta radio personality, on the first career triple of Greg Maddux*

Twins

"They take everything they can get and give nothing in return."

—ROD CAREW, *on negotiating with Twins management*

U

Umpires

"How could he be doing his job when he didn't throw me out of the game after the things I called him?"

—MARK BELANGER, *on umpire Russ Goetz*

"I never questioned the integrity of an umpire—their eyesight . . . yes."

—LEO DUROCHER

"He should concentrate on improving his record and let the umpires do their job."

—BRUCE FROEMMING, *umpire, on pitcher Jeff Fassero, who criticized an umpire*

"Anytime I got them bang-bang plays at first base, I called them out. It made the game shorter."

—TOM GORMAN

"When I am right, no one remembers. When I am wrong, no one forgets."

—DOUG HARVEY

"The way we have been playing, I might tell my players not to cross the picket line."

—WHITEY HERZOG, *on the 1979 umpires' strike*

"Well, then I think you are doing a lousy job."

—CLEON JONES, *after Jones asked an umpire if he could get thrown out of the game for what he was thinking and the umpire said no*

"Umpire's heaven is a place where he works third base every game. Home is where the heartache is."

—RON LUCIANO

"Throwing people out of a game is like learning to ride a bicycle—once you get the hang of it, it can be a lot of fun."

—RON LUCIANO

"I cursed him in Spanish and he threw me out in English."

—LOU PINIELLA, *on being thrown out of a game by umpire Armando Rodriguez*

"If a player doesn't do his job, he is sent to the minors. If umpires don't do their job, they just pack their bags and go to the next city."

—JOE TORRE

"I was shocked at the language he used. He suggested there had not been a marriage in my family for three generations."

—BILL VALENTINE, *umpire, on arguing with Alvin Dark*

"I don't say the umpiring is bad in our league [American], but we'd be better off playing on the honor system."

—DICK WILLIAMS

"Ed, you're the second-best umpire in the league. The other 23 are tied for first."

> —CARL YASTRZEMSKI, *joking with umpire Ed Runge*

Utility Man

"They're about to change our name to the Cleveland Light Company. We don't have anything but utility men."

> —LOU CAMILLI

"I have so many splinters from sitting on the bench that if somebody struck a match, I might catch fire."

> —BILL GRABARKEWITZ

"The whole thing is a laugh. . . . I mean, there was a bidding war for the Wonder Dog."

> —REX HUDLER, *nicknamed Wonder Dog, on signing with the Phillies*

"Let's see, that means you played in 301 innings."

—DUANE JOSEPHSON, *to utility man Frank Quilici, playing in his 300th major-league game*

V

Mike Vail

"There isn't enough money in the world to get me to manage if I had to look at that face every day."

—HERMAN FRANKS, *on Mike Vail*

Bobby Valentine

"Bobby is an arrogant [bleep] and he doesn't have to be, because he's a good manager. But he's an arrogant [bleep]."

—SPARKY ANDERSON

"It's closer to 100 percent than it is to 50 percent."

> —DALLAS GREEN, *on the percentage of people in baseball who do not respect Bobby Valentine*

Andy Van Slyke

"Andy is just visiting here. In two years, they're going to call him back to wherever it is he came from."

> —RICH DONNELLY, *on Andy Van Slyke*

Mo Vaughn

"Vaughn couldn't hit a high ball if you gave him eight bats up there."

> —SPARKY ANDERSON, *on Mo Vaughn early in his career*

Veterans Stadium

"It's a toll call if you want to talk to somebody at the other end. In fact, it's a different area code."

—RICK WISE, *on the clubhouse in Veterans Stadium*

W

Weapons

"In case somebody charged the mound."

> —RANDY MYERS, *on carrying a knife in one pocket and a two-foot chain in the other*

Weather Vane

"It ain't the heat, it's the humility."

> —YOGI BERRA

"Admiral Byrd threw out the first pitch."

> —ROCKY BRIDGES, *on an opening day in Buffalo*

"I don't think I should be asked to catch when the temperature is below my age."

> —CARLTON FISK, *on playing on a cold day when he was 43*

"What I want to know is when do the locusts come?"

> —PHIL GARNER, *after the Brewers were rained out, snowed out, and flooded out of several games*

"I was downgraded from a hurricane to a tropical depression."

> —REX HUDLER, *nicknamed Hurricane, after being released during the off-season*

"We had some days we had to pipe in the sun."

> —TOMMY LASORDA, *on playing in Pittsburgh*

"Don't pray when it rains if you don't pray when the sun shines."

> —SATCHEL PAIGE

"We got to freeze our butts and get them kicked at the same time."

> —LOU PINIELLA, *on the Mariners losing 20–3 on a 38-degree day*

"It's so cold out there, I saw a dog chasing a cat and they were both walking."

> —MICKEY RIVERS

Earl Weaver

"He's not happy unless he's unhappy."

> —ELROD HENDRICKS, *on Earl Weaver*

"I don't want to win my 300th game while he's still here. He'll take credit for it."

> —JIM PALMER, *on Earl Weaver*

"The first time Joe said hello to some guys, he broke Earl Weaver's career record."

> —JIM PALMER, *on Joe Altobelli replacing Earl Weaver as the Orioles' manager*

Weighty Issues

"There are only two things that will prevent him from greatness—a knife and a fork."

—FRANK LANE, *on Boog Powell*

"I have to watch my playing weight. But the problem is that I don't know what my playing weight is. I never play."

—JOE LIS

"This isn't a body. It's a cruel family joke."

—CURT SCHILLING, *on his weight*

"I'm admitting that I'm not in as good a shape as I was last year. But it's not that I'm a blob."

—MATT STAIRS

"I don't need a chest protector. I need a bra."

—GUS TRIANDOS, *overweight former catcher, on catching at an old-timers' game*

"There's one guy who spends all his meal money. None of it gets mailed home."

—BOBBY VALENTINE, *on Barry Foote*

David Wells

"At nighttime, you just try to keep him out of jail."

—DAVID CONE, *on David Wells*

"We have a pitcher from Cuba, from Japan, and from Panama, and Boomer Wells is from Mars."

—TINO MARTINEZ, *on the Yankees pitching staff*

White Sox

"Our 1976 White Sox team was so bad that by the fifth inning, Bill Veeck was selling hot dogs to go."

—KEN BRETT

"It's like a cemetery—a bunch of dead dogs."

—JAIME NAVARRO, *on the '98 White Sox*

Mitch Williams

"We know a ticker-tape parade wouldn't do well, because the tallest building in town is two stories."

> —SANDRA ETHRIDGE, *mayor of Mico, Texas, the hometown of Mitch Williams, on throwing a big party for Williams after the Phillies won the World Series*

"He doesn't have ulcers, but he's one of the biggest carriers there is."

> —JIM FREGOSI, *on Mitch Williams*

"If you're going to shoot yourself, do it in your room, not here [clubhouse]. You might miss and hurt someone."

> —JOHN KRUK, *to Mitch Williams after Williams nearly blew a game*

"If everyone was like him, I wouldn't play. I'd find a safer way to make a living."

> —ANDY VAN SLYKE, *on Mitch Williams*

Stan Williams

"In all the years I played, he was the only guy who ever scared me, and he was on my team."

—RON FAIRLY, *on Stan Williams*

Ted Williams

"If he'd just tip his cap once, he could be elected mayor of Boston in five minutes."

—EDDIE COLLINS, *on Ted Williams*

Wins

"You can't win every time. There are guys out there who are better than you are."

—YOGI BERRA

"Yeah, I'm pretty good on 670 days of rest."

—JOE MAGRANE, *on not being able to pitch for almost two years and picking up a win*

"It only took me 21 runs and five years to get a win here."

> —ANDY PETTITTE, *on his first win against the Rangers in Texas, a game the Yankees won by a score of 21–3*

World Series

"We're looking for four and out—the faster it's over with, the better it is for us."

> —DON OHLMEYER, *NBC executive, on the '97 World Series between the Marlins and the Indians*

World Tour

"Who are we going to play next, Iraq?"

> —BOBBY COX, *on the Orioles playing in Cuba*

"Frankly, I'd prefer someplace else."

> —BABE HERMAN, *after Charles Ebbets offered him a trip around the world*

"The U.S. is pretty clear. They have a very firm policy. We'll return to Cuba any Cuban who can't pitch."

> —DAVID LETTERMAN, *on the Clinton administration's efforts to return Elian Gonzales to Cuba*

Wrigley Field

"Instead of going to nightclubs, you go to happy hour."

> —GARY MATTHEWS, *on adjusting to playing during the day at Wrigley Field*

"I favor blowing this place up."

> —KEITH MORELAND, *when asked if he favored night games at Wrigley Field*

"I'd play for half my salary if I could hit in this dump all the time."

> —BABE RUTH, *on Wrigley Field*

X-Rays

"I've had so many X-rays that my pitches might take on a subtle glow."

—JOE MAGRANE

Y

Yankee Stadium

"I don't want to go to Yankee Stadium. I would have to arm myself."

> —GEORGE W. BUSH, *on the Rangers playing the Yankees in the playoffs*

"There's no way they can bury 12 people out there."

> —BOB KEARNEY, *on the 12 monuments at Yankee Stadium*

"I'd have rather been in a ring with 15 pit bulls and no clothes on."

> —CLYDE WRIGHT, *on his fear of pitching at Yankee Stadium*

Yankees

"As long as I'm around playing baseball, it doesn't matter where I am, as long as it's not with the Yankees."

> —CARL EVERETT

"A fatal attraction."

> —REGGIE JACKSON, *on the relationship between Billy Martin and George Steinbrenner*

"The Yankees are America's team. You know—mom, apple pie, Gucci loafers, Rolls-Royces . . ."

> —TOMMY JOHN

"If Billy goes undefeated, they'll get along fine."

> —MICKEY MANTLE, *when asked how he thought Billy Martin and George Steinbrenner would get along*

"The two of them deserve each other. One's a born liar, the other's convicted."

> —BILLY MARTIN, *on Reggie Jackson and George Steinbrenner*

"You can now call us the South Bronx Striders."

> —GRAIG NETTLES, *on Steinbrenner forcing the Yankees in spring training to wear sweat suits and run*

"When I was a kid, I wanted to play baseball and join the circus. With the Yankees, I've been able to do both."

> —GRAIG NETTLES

Yankees Fans

"They never let up on you. They have no courtesy at all. They're obnoxious. The worst."

> —BILL RUSSELL, *on Yankees fans*

"Things are definitely getting better, but I still check my mail for ticking."

> —ED WHITSON, *on his relationship with Yankees fans*

Carl Yastrzemski

"I wish they'd move him to first base. I get tired of running all the way over there in the outfield all the time to cover for him."

—FRED LYNN, *on Carl Yastrzemski, later in his career*

Youth Movements

"They're great—if you're a part of them."

—RICK MONDAY, *waived after 18 years in the majors, on youth movements*

Index

Italicized page numbers indicate names referred to in a quote. All other names are actual sources of a quote.

★ **M** ★